Huddle Up
and
cuddle up.

Dad is gone. You and your kids are experiencing feelings of alienation, depression, and disillusionment. As Gloria Chisholm says, "Go ahead—fall into each other's arms and grieve. You've got good reason to." But as you do this, be comforted in the knowledge that you still have each other— and God's healing Presence — as you move through the pain together.

In these pages, you'll discover that security, hope, joy, and peace can be reestablished in your home and in the heart of every family member. Be assured that you will not only survive but thrive when you *Huddle Up* together.

HUDDLE UP

GLORIA CHISHOLM

Fleming H. Revell Company
Tarrytown, New York

Library of Congress Cataloging-in-Publication Data

Chisholm, Gloria.
    Huddle up / Gloria Chisholm.
      p. cm.
    ISBN 0-8007-5410-7
    1. Single parents—United States. 2. Parent and child—United States. 3. Single parents—United States—Religious life. 4. Single mothers—United States.   I. Title.
HQ759.915.C48   1991
306.85'6—dc20   91-14228
                                                 CIP

CONTENTS

INTRODUCTION

What is a single parent? According to my kids, it's someone who:

- Has all the answers
- Has all the goods
- Has all the money
- Has all the time
- Has all the energy

. . . and all the love in the world. I haven't told them any differently. I, for one, have a difficult time with disappointment and disillusionment. If possible, I want my kids to experience them in small doses.

Now maybe they've discovered on their own that the above is not true or only partially true (I do have an awful lot of love).

The above definition is a nice fantasy for my kids. But closer to the truth, a single parent is someone who:

- Trains her kids
- Disciplines her kids
- Plays with her kids
- Hurts with her kids
- Laughs with her kids
- Guts it through life with her kids

. . . all alone. By all alone, I mean there is no other adult with whom to share the ups and downs, the highs and lows of parenting. No one else is around to help us gauge how we're doing.

It's depressing at times, and lonely—so lonely.

Reading a book on single parenting will not make the lonely times disappear; reading *this* book on single parenting will not make the lonely times disappear. But in the following pages, together we will discover ways to make the lonely times less lonely. It's possible—if you can avoid the natural tendency toward isolation of family members from one another and put your efforts into the formation of one unit that works for each individual.

We've been told that a primary goal of a family should be to get everyone on the same team. However, in a team, the emphasis is on the group or corporate body rather than on the individual. The definition of teamwork, according to Webster, is "a joint action by a group of people in which individual interests are subordinated to group unity and efficiency."

I would like to suggest that as single parents, we form a "unit." A *unit* is a single person (regarded as an individual but belonging to an entire group) or group, as distinguished from others or as part of a whole. The word *unit* is derived from *unity*, which is something united and complete in itself.

Is it worth the energy and effort to form a unit with your kids? Why not just leave them alone and let everybody try their best to survive this trip?

Because we all know that a ride is much smoother (I don't care if you're on a donkey or a speedboat) when everyone is exerting the same amount of energy and pulling in the same direction with the same destination in mind.

As single parents, we have a purpose: to raise our kids on a daily basis so that they, too, might discover God's purpose for their lives.

Sound like a lot of work? It is, but it's worth it, especially when my kids and I are united in purpose.

It's within the realm of possibility. Read on.

HUDDLE
✥ UP ✥

1
WE'RE IN THIS TOGETHER

When the Reality of Single Parenting Sets In

Ray backed the car out of the driveway and headed down the street toward church. I glanced around our station wagon and took a quick head count once again: one, two, three, four, five. Seven, if you counted Ray and me.

This is a family, I thought happily. *I'm part of a family with a dad, mom, and five beautiful kids.* And they were perfect—well, at least they looked that way when they were all dressed up for church. I'd remembered to check five heads of hair and five faces before we got out the door.

I loved the security of family life. My mother and father divorced when I was two years old, and my mother raised me alone—no brothers and sisters. My dad died when I was five; my mother never remarried. I spent day after day of my childhood alone.

I sighed contentedly. *This is how it's supposed to be. A dad, mom, kids. . . .*

Exactly one year later, we piled into the station wagon for church, as before. Head count: one, two, three, four,

five. Six, counting me. On closer inspection, I saw I'd
missed one head of hair and two faces. One holey pair of
pants, too. I sighed, only it wasn't in contentment this
time.

Someone was missing. It was evident everywhere. I
was divorced. A single parent. Overnight, I'd become a
statistic.

I Can't Believe It

"But I don't even believe in divorce."

"I don't have any money, no job—nothing."

"This can't be happening. No, I'll wake up from this
nightmare soon."

But every morning when I woke up, we were all still
there, the kids and I—and he was gone.

Life moves awfully slowly when you're waiting for
someone to bail you out of an impossible situation. I ag-
onized through long day after long day.

No one rescued me. And somehow, refusing to believe
it was happening didn't make it stop happening.

Numbness. Shock cushions the blows. When you first
stub your toe or hit your head, shock paralyzes you, but
then the pain registers and the throbbing can quickly drive
you crazy. Have you ever hurt so bad that you knew if you
hurt one more minute you'd die? I didn't want to feel that
kind of pain, so I stayed in a state of self-anesthetized
shock for a very long time.

How did I deal with a situation so much bigger than I
was? How did I get a perspective? After all, only one person had left my life. Why should it be so hard to live
without one person? I lived without him just fine before I
met him.

Those were the wrong questions to ask. You can't analyze pain at the moment it's ripping your heart open.

While trying to deal with my own pain, I had to deal with five little people who needed lots of attention, especially now.

"Mom, will you put my basketball hoop up for me?"

It took too long, but I did it.

"Mom, hold me."

Hug after hug after hug after hug. Clinging, whining. Is there such a thing as too many hugs? How can I hold five kids all the time?

"Mom, I need—"

"No!" I screamed. "No! I don't care what you need."

But that's not what I meant to say, and it was so untrue.

Time passed (weeks? months? I'd lost track) and the numbness began to wear off. When I thought about it, I realized I'd been numb for much longer than I'd thought.

I awakened to the pain and looked frantically for the way out. God's answer was not to reach down and lift me out. No, it was to walk me through. *Rats.* I gritted my teeth. It got worse. I tried to relax. It got worse. I decided that I'd rather not do this, after all. It's like that step into the hospital delivery room: You can't change your mind; the only way out is through.

How did I get here? I still can't believe it. It took two of us to create these little ones (who are growing into bigger ones at an alarming rate). How did I end up raising them alone?

We moms fall into a solo parenting role through one of many avenues, none of which is pleasant. The most common may be through divorce. Or our husbands die, leaving us and our kids in the throes of grief. Some experience the trauma of rape, and rather than going the abortion/

adoption route, decide to keep the child. Some bear children outside marriage and for reasons in or out of their control, stay unmarried.

How you got into this place, as unbelievable and traumatizing as it may be, soon becomes a lesser issue as you fight for survival. At least it should become a lesser issue. If you struggle with the whys, past regrets, how you could have prevented it, and so forth for too long, you'll move into nonproductive grief.

As I see it, when things like this hit, you can really only deal with life in two basic ways:

• Laugh in its face
• Curl up in a corner somewhere to die

Okay, that may sound a bit oversimplified. Even with these two choices, we have many options, and God is extremely creative in how He chooses to take us through, once we give Him the reins. We're in this together: God, me, and the kids—once I get past the rage, the fear, and the grief.

The Rage

I wasn't prepared for the inner rage at this turn of events in my life. I wonder if Paul was thinking about single moms when he wrote, "Let not the sun go down upon your wrath" (Ephesians 4:26 KJV). I'm afraid the sun came and went regularly, and my wrath refused to budge.

Divorce is one thing. This isn't a book about divorce. Divorced and left with five little people is quite another thing. That's what this book is about.

You bet I was mad! Enraged! The way it must feel to invest thousands of dollars in the stock market and watch it all go down the tubes in a weekend. No, it's worse than that, because you're left with much more than a stack of useless stock certificates.

"Mom, how come you're always frowning?"

"Mom, you mad at me?"

"Mom, what would make you happy again?"

They didn't have to say anything. Living with me was like living with Mount St. Helens. We lived under a layer of volcanic ash from my frequent eruptions.

Anger turned to bitterness. What now? No one could stop Mount St. Helens, and no one could stop me.

Life had ceased to be fun. Had it ever been fun? I looked at my kids. I looked at my rage. I'd never been this route before; I didn't know what to do.

Kids have such a simple way of dealing with their anger. I came home from work one day to find Dwight, surrounded by tools, busily twisting a screw into his skateboard.

"How was your day?" he asked, not looking up from his task.

"Terrible. I'm having a problem with some people at work."

"Waste 'em," he advised, still intent on his skateboard.

"You mean, waste 'em?"

"Yeah." He chuckled. "Waste 'em."

Waste 'em? Just beat 'em up? Of course. Why didn't I think of that? It's so simple: Just pound anyone who gets in your way.

I didn't follow through, but I did enjoy entertaining the thought for a moment.

What do we do with the rage? I'm not the only one who's mad, either. My kids got ripped off, too. So did yours.

Find an appropriate way to express it.

"Yeah, sure," you say. The refrigerator stopped working. Stevie brought a pink slip home from school (I hate
those pink slips. If I were a teacher, the first thing I'd do
is tear up my pink slips), and Julie just told you she hated
you because her new white blouse turned pale blue in the
wash.

"Aaaaargh!" is all you can get out some days. But the
rage is always just under the surface, waiting to boil over,
and the one who deserves it (your ex, boss, or abuser) is
never the one who gets it. Sad.

What to do? What are your options?

- Borrow an old stuffed animal from your kids and
  pummel him regularly or whenever an explosion
  seems imminent.
- Whine and complain incessantly to all your friends
  about how your life is ruined.
- Get in your car, roll up the windows, and scream
  and cry until your rage is spent.

Go ahead—express it. Encourage your kids to express it.
You're in this together. Huddle—now cry, scream, really
gut out. Let the anger go from deep down.

Anger gives way to fear. They vie for first place in your
emotional realm.

The Fear

"No way!" you cry. "I can't do this!"

Then this paralyzing, terrifying panic begins to rise from
the core of your being. Your stomach knots and your heart
contracts. You're scared to death.

"Hey, Mom, whatsa' matter? You been reading Stephen

King again? You look like you just watched a hatchet murder."

Through eyes wide with fear, you stare at your tall (at least a head taller than you), raggedy-jeaned, tousle-haired teenage son, the same son you've already lived with for fifteen years. But now you alone are responsible for him. What if he takes drugs? Drinks and drives? Gets his girlfriend pregnant? What if he falls off his skateboard and breaks his neck? What about college? How will you afford it? What if he decides he no longer wants to eat his vegetables? What if he joins a street gang?

The terror moves into your throat and threatens to choke you.

"How can you do this to me?" you cry. "How can you put me through all this torment after all I've done for you?"

He shakes his head, shrugs, and goes outside to shoot baskets, just as he does every day.

If it's a toddler in a playpen stuffing graham crackers into his mouth, you're looking at about seventeen years of responsibility.

How do you deal with this kind of irrational fear? Obviously, it's out of your control.

Our fears concerning our kids are valid. Ted Bundy, the serial killer, was his mother's child. Every prison in this country is full of men and women who were once little boys and girls like yours and mine.

Are the mothers responsible? If so, why weren't they sentenced along with their children? No, people make choices. Your kids will make wrong choices sometimes—you can count on it. Knowing that doesn't make a mother's heart hurt any less when it happens, but it does alleviate the sense of guilt and responsibility that we often bear unnecessarily.

Let's examine our fears in the broad light of day while our teenage sons shoot baskets and our toddlers coo in their playpens.

Here are the top ones:

- We'll do something wrong regarding our kids, and they will hate and reject us.
- We'll do something wrong regarding our kids, and society, the kids' father, and our friends and neighbors will blame and reject us.
- We'll do something wrong regarding our kids, and God will punish and reject us.

Lined up like that, we can see what we're really afraid of. The fear of death also enters into the picture if we can't provide enough food or pay the rent. Big fears, understandable fears, scary fears.

But we're in this together.

"Hey, Mom, I'm scared."

Let's remember that our kids are scared, too. Scared of things that go bump in the night; scared of schoolteachers and tests; scared of menstrual periods, acne, sexual feelings, growing up. They're even scared of moms sometimes.

Whew! It's a rough ride. I wish the end of the anger and fear stages marked the end of our pain. Unfortunately we have yet to grieve this sad state of affairs.

The Grief

"You will grieve, but your grief will turn to joy" (John 16:20).

If I didn't believe this Scripture, I don't know where I would find the courage to enter into the pain of grief.

Jesus said these words to His disciples as they were about to lose Him to the cross. He knew their grief would feel hopeless at times.

Like anger and fear, grief must be expressed so it can run its course.

Not knowing any better, I only began to grieve the end of my marriage a few months ago, and it's been six years since my divorce.

"Mom, why are your cheeks wet?" A tiny hand reached up to brush away a tear.

Even as I write this, I wonder if I've made a place for my kids to grieve the separating of their mommy and daddy. I must do that as soon as possible.

We're in this together. We must grieve together that we might comfort one another.

As mothers, we grieve:

- The loss of our dreams
- The loss of relationship
- The loss (or hope) of support and sharing in the raising of our children
- A passing era

"Mom, it's Father's Day tomorrow, remember?"

No, you didn't. You had tried to forget. Now what? Go ahead—fall into each other's arms and grieve. You've got good reason to.

To grieve is to:

- Let go of the pain so it doesn't poison you on the inside
- Let life's disappointments impact you, so you can feel and empathize with the hurt of others
- Hurt with and for your kids in the loss of their

father as they knew him or might have known him
- "Participate in the sufferings of Christ, so that you may be overjoyed when his glory is revealed" (1 Peter 4:13)

"Mom, are you smiling yet?"

The Acceptance

Yes, a smile is appearing on the horizon. We might survive this blow, after all.

I knew I'd come a long way the day someone said the word *family* and I identified instead of feeling ostracized. It's not we were "once" a family or we "will be" a family if I remarry. No, we *are* a family.

Until we accept our circumstances, we can't move through the pain. Jesus sweated drops of blood in the Garden of Gethsemane, so great was his anguish. His moment of acceptance came when He cried, "Father, if you are willing, take this cup from me; yet not my will, but yours be done" (Luke 22:42).

In the same way, although our flesh cries out for relief from this cup of single parenting, can we accept God's will, whatever it might be?

Acceptance is:

- Calling a cease-fire to the attacks on the missing member of your unit
- Knowing you're okay—as okay as the family next door with the dad who mows the lawn and leads his family in evening devotions
- Rolling up your sleeves and tackling the assemblage of the mountain bike you bought your son for his birthday

- Maintaining your sanity when your daughter screams about how rotten it is now compared to how wonderful it all was when "Dad was here"
- Knowing God loves and wants to care for you and your kids, with or without a male in the picture

"Mom, you're in a good mood. Hey, can I have a quarter? I hear the ice-cream man."

We're single moms. We must cease fighting that. Instead, we must use our energy to fight the mentality that says we're "less than" because someone is missing. Once we accept what is, we can redirect our energies toward positive growth.

The Hope

I can tell when my kids are hopeless: They go to bed in the middle of the day. When I'm hopeless, I stop caring a whole lot. I feel myself go numb inside. Sharp pain turns to dull ache. Activity stops.

How is hope reactivated? We first need to understand where hope originates.

Our hope doesn't lie in:

- Getting the uncooperative party to return to the scene of the crime
- Finding a high-paying job so we can provide all our children's needs and wants
- Finding another man to replace the missing family member
- Breaking our backs to be both mother and father to our children
- Denying and sacrificing ourselves that our kids might have everything to compensate for their missing father

• Trying to play God in our kids' lives

Our hope lies in one relationship and one relationship only: "The God of hope [who fills] you with all joy and peace as you trust in him, so that you may overflow with hope by the power of the Holy Spirit" (Romans 15:13).

We've moved through unbelief, anger, fear, and grief. We've accepted our single-parenting role and are trusting God to redeem the past. We know that in our relationship with Him lies our hope for our future and the future of our kids.

"Mom, are we using the same road map?"

Forming the Unit

Under the stress of single parenting, unless we mothers decide to bond with our kids, we'll automatically enter into an adversarial relationship with them. And without our kids on our side, we are in for an extremely rough and painful parenting ride.

Now's the time to think about forming the aforementioned unit. It's a matter of constant recommitment for all. You need them—they need you. The minute you sense one of you becoming the enemy, stand back and get a perspective. What's wrong?

This is not a book about learning how to "control" your kids now that you're left alone to raise them. It's not a book about "surviving" single parenthood. Its purpose is not to teach you how to raise "perfect kids," for we have no guarantees. We're humans.

Well, if it's not about gaining control, surviving single parenthood, or raising better kids, then what is it about?

It's about giving up control, enjoying single parenthood,

and raising normal kids. The only way to do that is to relax our grip around their necks and join hands with them.

They may or may not choose to walk with us. They may or may not choose to stay close. Whatever, it is as much their choice as it is ours.

That's the only way to walk with our kids—by choice—theirs and ours. God likes that kind of stuff. That's why He gave Adam and Eve the freedom of choice.

We're in this together—same road map, same game rules.

"Hey, Mom, is it your move or mine?"

Neither. Both. It's ours.

2
BUT I DON'T FEEL LIKE IT

Meeting Demands When You're Out of Energy

"Mom, I need a present for Katie's party on Saturday. Oh, and we're going on a field trip Thursday. I need this permission slip signed and four-fifty."

Amber trips up the stairs at that point, crying, "Dwight won't let me watch cartoons. He says they're stupid. He turned the channel."

Dwight appears around the corner. "They are stupid. I was watching something first—"

"Liar!"

In the background I note dirty dishes stacked to the ceiling. Coats and school papers are strewn across the floor, dropped by their owners at random. I'm semiconscious of Dwight's voice droning on and Amber's high-pitched screech in reaction. I've only been home from work for two minutes. A typical scene on any given day.

One of two things usually happens next.

"Leave me alone!" I scream and burst into frustrated

tears. Or I numbly ignore them and retreat to my bed-room, where I burst into frustrated tears.

When I get home from work, that's it. I'm it. Daddy will not arrive shortly after to help me love and care for the individual needs of the parts of our unit, or to love and care for me.

The demands of parenthood are overwhelming. The demands on a single parent are double. And if you have more than one kid—you get the picture.

Do you always feel like being your kid's parent? Do you ever have days when you'd rather be an important executive on Wall Street? Or a Hollywood producer? A circus clown, maybe? Anybody other than the one responsible for the little person you tuck into bed each night? C'mon, be honest; we all have days like that. Why? There are too many demands and not enough energy. Add feelings of failure to the depleted energy, and you've got an unhappy family relationship. If we want to form a "united front"—a unit, if you please—everyone (including me) must become aware of their demandingness, take responsibility for it, and be willing to carry their share of the load.

Demands

Let's look at this from the kid's point of view.

At five years old: "I want a cookie." *Mommy will give me a cookie.*

"No, dear, not before dinner."

"I want a cookie now." *Mommy will give me a cookie. I always get what I want.*

"No, dear. It'll spoil your supper."

Stomps foot. "Give me a cookie!" *And hurry up. Why do we always have to go through this?*

"No, dear. I told you, it will—"

"Waaa!" *Too bad I have to resort to this.*

"Oh, all right."

Smiles. *I knew it.*

At ten years old: Same scenario, only it's not a cookie, but time, attention, energy. And the "waaa!" becomes a slammed door.

At fifteen years old: Same scenario, only this time it's a cookie, time, attention, energy, and everything else in between. And the "waaa!" becomes running away from home or a closed heart.

And we bear the brunt alone.

Do the demands ever let up? I'm not sure. But we can minimize their stress if we can learn to discern between legitimate requests and outrageous demands. Too often the problem is that it even takes energy to stop and discern, but it gets easier and becomes more automatic the more we do it.

One thing to remember: You can't let your children's demands run your life. (To be fair, we must also make sure that we're not trying to run their lives with our outrageous demands.) But they may threaten to do just that, because our children know how to get us to plug into guilt.

What is an outrageous demand?

"Mom, Pete's selling a Nintendo game for only twenty dollars. I need it tonight, before he sells it to someone else. Duckhunt—can you believe it?—for only twenty dollars. It sells for forty dollars in the store. What a lucky break. Anyway, do you need to go to the bank or anything before it closes?"

Or, "Mom, I know you said I could have eight people at my birthday party, but I need to have a few more, because all these kids in my class found out that we're going to Wild Waves and they want to come and I hate to hurt their feelings. I know you wouldn't want me to do that—it's a bad witness—and anyway, I need to have about twenty-five."

I know someone who had an overnighter for her son's tenth birthday and let him invite sixty kids. She did it again when he was eighteen. She and her husband *wanted* to do it as a gift to their son, making it less stressful than if he'd demanded it and they'd permitted it out of guilt.

Not having an extra twenty bucks hanging around, either in my purse or in the bank, I didn't *want* to purchase the used Nintendo game, such a great deal. And I certainly didn't *want* to invite twenty-five kids to my son's birthday party. My sanity is worth something, since I've worked so hard at it for so long, and I'd hate to lose it in a moment at a birthday party, of all places.

It's an outrageous demand when:

- Your child must have it, have it now, and will not take no for an answer
- To meet the demand would cause you undue pressure, either financially (the video game) or emotionally (the twenty-five kids)

"No."

"No? What do you mean 'no'?" Yells, screams, manipulation, threats; I've ruined his life.

It's a legitimate request when:

- Your child asks something of you that she can take or leave and offers you the choice of whether to do it or not (I know, dream on)

- You don't feel manipulated and granting the request would make the child truly grateful

Okay, so we're looking at the ideal. It never hurts to compare or measure the ideal against the real to see how far off everyone is.

It's not that we have to "feel like" doing everything. We do much for our kids that we don't want to do or don't feel like doing, but because the demands are so unyielding, the more we do because we want to, the less we'll resent our kids and the less energy it will take. So much of our stress comes from what we perceive as pressure, a lack of choice in the matter, and feelings of being trapped.

This is true for our kids, as well. As I mentioned above, parents are also capable and guilty of making outrageous demands, especially single parents, because we do not have another adult with whom to share the load. In a healthy family everyone is accountable to everyone else for their demandingness. We can confront one another.

Responses

I read in a woman's magazine once that living with kids is a series of demands and responses. If you don't believe that, I assume you don't have kids, or are hard-of-hearing.

It never ceases to amaze me how each one of my kids, although he or she has contact with many different people each day, seems to think that the world actually revolves around him or her and no one else.

When my kid has a need, it's *always* urgent, and I can too easily fall into that demand-response syndrome if I'm not careful. Since I'm it, since there's no one else around eager to respond to my kids' demands, I have to weigh each demand and calculate the appropriate response.

When Paul wrote, "Do not be anxious about anything" (Philippians 4:6), I wonder if he was thinking about kids? When he wrote in the previous verse, "Let your gentleness be evident to all," I wonder if he was thinking about parents? How can I cultivate a gentle response to my kids when they're anxious so much of the time? Ninety percent of the time would be a safe estimate. A high estimate of my evident gentleness is probably five to ten percent of the time.

I figure I have only a few options, where my response to their demands is concerned. I can:

- Say I have to go to the bathroom, run to the bathroom, and climb out the window
- Scream and yell that I'm not a money machine, miracle worker, and so forth
- Tune them out and plan my next novel
- Smile wickedly and tell them their father has been wanting to hear from them
- Cry
- Pray like mad that God will keep me from wringing their little demanding necks

We all know that on TV the mother would pat her child's head and say sweetly, "Well, of course, dear, I'm sure we'll be able to send you to camp for five hundred dollars. Your father will get the money in the morning." Daddy nods and the child cheers, hugs his or her parents, and runs outside to tell his or her friends. The theme song plays, and all the television viewers feel great contentment.

I would like nothing better than to respond like a TV mother and give my child whatever he or she needs. Unfortunately, I don't have a husband with deep pockets to nod agreement.

Plus, I'm tired before the demands even begin. The desire to run threatens to overcome me. But I don't think my kids understand that. When they have a need, they like someone to be available.

I know how they feel.

"But you're an adult," one or the other of my kids is always telling me when we talk about needs. They mean that I'm supposed to be all grown-up about my needs. My pain couldn't be nearly as intense as theirs, my needs not nearly as great. Guess again. I keep telling them that it gets worse as we get older, not better. They're too into themselves to hear me.

I guess there is one more option that I left off the list of possible responses to demands: Without withdrawing physically, I can withdraw to a place inside myself that only God and I share. It takes only a moment for His peace to become mine.

"Hey, Mom, I need—"

Click. "Lord, give me Your peace, Your wisdom, Your strength, and Your kind of love that transcends all demands."

Guilt

Kids don't necessarily look as smart as they really are, so we tend to forget that underneath their innocent appearances are all kinds of clever, manipulative tactics to get us to do what they want—*now*.

How they have arrived at the grand conclusion that I am the one always available to all their needs and demands shouldn't be so hard to understand. It may go back to the first few years of their lives, when I was right there, popping a breast into their hungry little mouths every time they even whimpered and especially if they wailed. It's understandable that they could draw this conclusion about me. Anyone with a brain, even a small child's brain, could deduce that if their demands aren't being met, it could be only one person's fault. Guess who? Therefore, if we all agree on this, it's easy to imagine what is produced inside me if I fail to live up to my part of the deal. You guessed it—guilt. My sweet little imps know this and know how to plug into it whenever they need to.

My twelve-year-old runs into the house at five o'clock, screaming, "What's for dinner? I'm starved. I don't smell anything cooking." He screeches to a stop at the sight of me lying on the couch, a novel in my hand. His mouth drops open as if he'd just caught me naked or I'd just grown three heads. "What? You haven't even started it? What have you been doing all day?"

Before I have a moment to think, guilt kicks in. I jump up and race to the kitchen, where I frantically search the freezer for something, anything, to serve my starving child. I'm not even prepared. How dare I spend a leisurely Saturday reading when I knew five o'clock would come and my kids would be hungry? I'm not exactly the Proverbs 31 woman who "gets up while it is still dark; [and] provides food for her family" (Proverbs 31:15).

By the way, I hate the Proverbs 31 woman. I hate the way "her arms are strong for her tasks" (v. 17) when mine feel like limp dishrags most of the time. I hate the way "her lamp does not go out at night" (v. 18) when mine often begins to flicker as early as seven-thirty in the evening. And I really hate the way "she speaks with wisdom, and faithful instruction" (v. 26). I can barely moan at

the end of some days, let alone teach my children profound truths about life and God.

If my kids ever get hold of Proverbs 31, I've had it for
sure.

But the virtuous woman wasn't a single mom, either. In
one way, though, my singleness compounds the guilt.
Daddy-wise, my kids have gotten ripped off. Shouldn't I
spend every waking moment of every day trying to make
it up to them? That's what they'd like me to believe. No,
the absence of a father does not have to thrust me into a
prison of guilt.

So then what do I do with the guilt? Is it false guilt or
real guilt that causes me to feel as if I've committed a crime
whenever I've failed to meet, or failed to meet in time, or
haven't wanted to meet, one of my kids' demands?

Questions to ask myself the next time I "fail" one of my
children:

- Have I done anything wrong? According to whom?
- Are someone's expectations too high? Mine? My
  child's?
- What does God expect of me?

Laboring under guilt, real or false, is hard work. False
guilt is the enemy's weapon to further weaken our energy
as single parents. But real guilt brings conviction, after
which we need to repent and receive God's forgiveness. It
might help to remember that you didn't create these kids
by yourself, and the absence of the other party is not necessarily your fault. So is it up to you to meet every need,
demand, and expectation?

One thing about kids: No matter how much we do for
them, it's never enough.

Little Johnny opens sixty-five presents under the Christmas tree with his name on them. He then becomes frantic, diving wildly in and out of the shredded wrappings and gifts. "Where's my _____? I asked for a _____!" (You fill in the blanks.)

You've saved for a year to take the family on a much-looked-forward-to vacation. You go to Disneyland, Universal Studios, Magic Mountain, Knotts Berry Farm. You even drive over to Palm Springs to soak up some of the most beautiful sun in the country. All the way home, Little Susie pouts in a corner of the backseat of the car. "How come we didn't go to _____? You know how much I wanted to go to _____!"

Do you feel guilty? You might.

Guilt will rob you of the little bit of energy you've managed to hang onto in order to drag yourself out of bed each morning.

Once you've discerned whether your guilt is real or false, deal with it immediately. If it's real, repent. If it's false, get your unit back on track. Tell your kids that:

- You've given up guilt for Lent
- The complaint mode of your inner computer has moved into overload and it can't possibly handle any more data until the year 2025, at which time your munchkins will surely have munchkins of their own
- You've appreciated their input all these years as regards your role in their lives, but from here on out they're to write to Ann Landers—then give them her address

The more you can rid yourself of guilt, the more energy you'll have for what really matters—more guilt and the other attitudes that too easily surface when you're tired and "don't feel like it."

Attitudes

Nothing can deplete our energy more quickly than a negative or bad attitude. Maybe I don't want to wipe any more runny noses, play hide-and-seek with any more missing shoes, or drive sixteen miles across town through rush-hour traffic to pick up my son at soccer practice. Some days I don't want to do this stuff, that's all. And I'm not one bit nice about it.

You can tell you need an attitude check when:

- Your temperature registers 105 degrees and you're not sick
- You keep threatening to send your oldest to Uncle Harry's for the summer, and your oldest keeps asking why he's never heard of Uncle Harry before now
- You find yourself grinding your teeth in your sleep so loudly that you wake yourself up

An attitude, according to Webster, is a manner of acting, feeling, or thinking that shows one's disposition, opinion, and so forth. It often grows so subtly that I'm unaware of it until one of my kids pipes up to another, "Hey, I'd say Mom has an attitude problem." The consensus is always unanimous.

Some might think it's disrespectful for kids to tell their parents they have an attitude problem, but if my kids don't tell me, who will? When my attitude problems expose themselves, I don't have a husband who:

- Gets a wounded look on his face

- Laughs and says, "You're cute when you're mad."
- Goes to sleep in the den because the atmosphere in the bed is icy cold

My kids' help is one of the benefits of the unit, so I won't become a crotchety old lady at thirty-eight.

Unlike a physical illness, an attitude problem cannot be treated with medication. Nor can it be shoved to a back shelf of the closet or taken to a mechanic for repairs.

But, as with a body or a car, maintenance is the key. Attitude problems within the family can be prevented. How?

We Can Lower Our Expectations

What do I mean by that? Does that mean that when I give Grant his first BB gun I expect him to shoot everybody's pet dog and cat and a few neighbor kids to boot, so that when he only shoots out someone's window, I'm thrilled? Not exactly.

It does mean that I can't expect my house to stay spotless; a little bit of kid dirt and clutter is okay. They'll all be gone soon enough, and then I know I'll miss the clutter that says kids live here.

It does mean that the most I can expect from my kids is that they be the little humans they are. I should be able to expect more from my ten-year-old than from my eight-year-old but won't count on it. Each child is different.

It does mean that I can expect my kids to sin because they're sinners, which leads us to the next preventative step for warding off attitude problems.

We Can Offer Forgiveness Instead of Pigeonholing

It's so easy to take my son, whose bedroom you enter at your own risk, put him in a box, and label it "disorganized." Or label my daughter, who has a tendency to want everyone and everything to revolve around her, "self-centered."

But if I forgive each offense, each demand, as it occurs, I can prevent making a judgment or forming a bad attitude toward my child.

"Hey, Mom, I got my report card today. I got a D in spelling."

Ouch. I was often the last one standing during the spelling bees in grade school. I'm a writer, after all. An attitude problem could start right here. "How humiliating—I've got a dumb kid." Or "I forgive you for that D (*one* D) in spelling. Can you try a little harder?"

Then—"God, give me the energy to spend a little bit of extra time with this child on his spelling."

Energy Sources

Can depleted energy be restored? Are we single parents doomed to lives of bone weariness because of the constant demands? Are we hopelessly optimistic to think we can ever rise above the tiredness? I wondered about this as I watched the other members of the family bounce tirelessly through each day.

During the stress of my divorce, I probably slept ten to twelve hours a day. I cried every single day (a real energy sapper if the deep sorrow is nonproductive, and mine at that time was).

A year later, when I started working full-time, there were days when I was sure I was losing my sanity. I had never been so tired in my whole life. Hardly a day passed that I didn't fall asleep at my desk. I was tired when I awoke in the morning, tired when I got home from work in the afternoon (and still had to face the herd), tired when I fell into bed early each evening.

Yet, today, six years later, I have more energy than I've ever had. I sleep only six hours a night, and I never take naps. (Have you taken a nap since you've had kids? I'd like to know how you do it.) The truth is, I'm not tired, and my schedule is busier than ever.

Some people excuse themselves by saying, "Oh, you're just a high-energy person." But these people didn't know me during my divorce. God and I have worked hard to get me to this place, and I think we need a little credit. God knew that in order for my five kids and me to survive, I would have to learn some hard lessons. You've read all the following before, I know, but it's really true.

Extreme fatigue (the kind of fatigue that causes us to want to live in bed with the covers pulled over our heads) is caused by a few major/minor wrong beliefs. They're major because they can kill us; minor because they're within our control:

- We must do it all
- We must do it all perfectly
- We must please everyone (especially those little people in our homes)

Put these three beliefs together with the crisis of single parenting (it's an ongoing crisis, a life-style crisis that never really ends), and you could be ready for the men in white. Where's the hope?

The following is brought to you by one whose entire life could only be called a crisis. Ask my kids or my friends. No, on second thought, don't.

Our hope lies in knowing:

- We only have to do some of it
- It's impossible to do any of it perfectly

• We only have to please God (and ourselves if our
  hearts are one with His)

Since our very existence is what pleases God, not
whether we're "good" or "bad" or "perfect," we have it
made.

To apply this more specifically to single parenting:

• We can choose the demands we want to meet. What
  freedom!
• As single parents, imperfection is the norm. Everyone might as well get used to it.
• We must love our kids. Sometimes the expression
  of our love will please them, sometimes it won't.

Other than that, when I feel the demands press in, I
know I must:

• Withdraw to a lonely place and pray (*see* Luke 5:16)
• Lighten up—have fun

One of the phrases tossed around at my church a lot is
"Love Jesus and have fun." That's about what it boils
down to. Fortunately, the success of this simple approach
to life does not hinge on whether or not we have a daddy/
husband. Unfortunately, our kids may need to be convinced. What if they want a dad and want him now? What
if they hold us responsible for making that happen—
pronto? Hang on—the battle is on.

3
YOU WANT A WHAT?

When They Want a Dad—Any Kind

"What? You want a what?"

"A dad," eleven-year-old Grant repeated. "I want a dad—or a stepdad—or something. Brian's stepdad fixed my scooter today. He's nice." He reached into the kitchen cupboard, grabbed some crackers, and shoveled them into his mouth, hundreds of crumbs breaking off and dropping onto my freshly mopped linoleum. "So where have you been lookin'?"

"Lookin'?" I echoed numbly.

"Yeah—for a dad. You're lookin', aren't you?"

"Um, well. Yeah, sure. I mean, if something turns up, I'll let you know."

"If something turns up?" He eyed me suspiciously. "How hard are you lookin'?"

"Well, you can't just pull a dad off a shelf like you can a loaf of bread, you know."

"Of course, I know that. I'm not stupid. But you have to

look. It doesn't sound like you're even trying. You never talk about getting one."

"Grant, have you finished your homework?"

This conversation was making me increasingly nervous. The truth was, I wasn't actually looking and felt no inclination to do so in the near future. I *liked* being single, but somehow I didn't think Grant would understand if I told him that. And one thing about Grant: Once he got onto something, well, he was like a dog with a bone. Better to let him think I was putting forth some effort, making myself available, and all that.

"Yep, I'm all done," Grant answered my question. "Where are you lookin' this week?"

"Actually, Todd called yesterday."

"Oh, c'mon. Todd." Grant chuckled. "He doesn't count. He's not—well, you know—not exactly—"

"What you had in mind," I filled in.

"Right."

"And what did you have in mind?" *This ought to be interesting*, I thought. Seriously, what did this kid need that I wasn't giving him?

"Well, a guy, you know. . . ."

A guy. That was a good start.

"A guy that likes to work in the garage, likes to build stuff. A guy that likes animals, likes to play ball in the street. A guy that . . ." his voice broke. "A dad. I want a dad." He turned quickly and left the room.

I watched him go. I wanted to run after him and make the hurt go away. Instead, I decided to let him feel his pain, because nothing I could say would ease the hurt.

Grant loved magic tricks, but I couldn't pull a dad out of

a hat. Grant loved hammers and nails, but I couldn't build a dad out of plywood.

I was a writer, but I couldn't create a dad out of sheer imagination. Not a real one, and Grant needed a real one—the flesh-and-blood kind—the kind that wrestled you down to the ground and when you knew you couldn't go one more round, called out, "I've had enough. You win." The kind that woke up early on Saturday morning and wanted to go hiking or fishing or swimming. The kind that loved Batman, He-man, and Superman and didn't care who knew it. The kind that hugged.

Last night ten-year-old Merilee asked, "Mom, do you think we need a dad?"

"Nah. Do you?"

"Nah."

That was yesterday. It changes daily.

Some of us are looking and some of us are not.

Some of us are looking some of the time.

Some of us are looking all of the time.

The case of our looking status isn't what matters. What matters is how the family is doing on the contentment scale without one of those creatures called a daddy around.

When You're Lookin'

Let's face it right up front. I've talked to enough single parents to know that I'm in the minority; most of you are looking. You want:

- Someone to cuddle with at night
- Someone with whom to share your dreams and schemes
- Someone to love

Recently I've had some lonely times and have actually considered looking myself, so the other night I made a grand attempt and went to a singles group. A certain man, Roger, seemed interested until:

"Do you live alone?" I asked, making polite conversation.

"Yeah. Do you?"

"Not exactly. I have these five kids who insist on hanging around." I grinned.

Roger was choking on his cookie. It must have gone down the wrong pipe. "I guess we should be mingling," he finally said when he could talk again.

That was fine with me. I was tired of hearing about his latest love relationship gone sour; it was all he'd talked about for the last twenty minutes.

Of course, I report each of these attempts to my kids so they know I'm making an effort once in a while, feeble though it may be. They have no idea how feeble, and yet the interrogation begins.

"Did you kiss him?"

"Does he want to marry you?"

"Is he cute?"

"Does he like kids?"

I don't always know the answers, but it entertains everyone for a while and reassures my kids that I'm (semi) serious about this looking jazz. In short, it keeps them off my back.

I don't envy those of you single women who are more than semiserious about looking. It's not that easy, and with all the weirdos running around these days, it can even be a dangerous venture.

Besides, we can't leave our kids home every night while we go out on the prowl.

The solution, as I see it, is to merge the looking process as much as we can with everyday life. How? Following are some steps that might help.

Pray Every Day

Get God involved in the process at the beginning.

Many of us are so starved for love and affection that we grab the first available (or not-so-available) man walking down the street.

I'm not sure that we should pray for God to find us a marriage partner unless we're absolutely certain beyond any doubt that that's what's best for the family at the present time. Sometimes we're simply so terrified of being alone that we panic and grasp onto marriage as the only antidote to the pain of aloneness.

How about asking God to help us meet some male *friends* who would enhance our spiritual and emotional growth as women? God is more interested in our long-term character as people than He is in our finding a man to take care of us when we're afraid we can't take care of ourselves.

Often (maybe most often), when we're looking, we don't know what we're doing. Sometimes our emotions or hormones are what's leading us. James 1:5 tells us that if we lack wisdom, we should ask God and He'll give it to us. Further on in that chapter, he says that "every good and perfect gift is from above" (James 1:17). Truly, friendship with a man that leads to romance and eventually to marriage can be a good and perfect gift from above.

Stay cool. A relationship with a man can also be a diversion or detour from hell itself. We need wisdom.

Look Every Day

You never know what you may find just around the
corner.

"Mom, how come you're putting on makeup? We're
only going to the store."

You never know.

Sometimes I need help staying alert. Like Jesus' disciples, "The spirit is willing, but the body is weak" (Matthew 26:41).

Recently, my seventeen-year-old son and I went to the
store. As I approached the fish counter, I had one thing on
my mind: scallops and smelt.

"I'd like some smelt," I told the man behind the counter
as I eyed the plump fish in the glass case.

"Certainly." He whipped a piece of butcher paper out
from under the counter and spread it out with a flourish.

"Not bad, Mom," Travis whispered in my ear. "Cute
even. What do you think?"

I stared at the fish more closely. *Scaly maybe, but cute?*

"How many would you like?" the man asked.

Travis jabbed me in the ribs. My head shot up. *Oh, him!*
I thought as I woke up. *Yeah, not bad.*

"Well, I'm not sure. How many can one person eat?"

"Hey, I can put away ten or fifteen of these little dudes
on a good night. Do you have any—uh—men at home?"
He winked at Travis.

Before I could answer, another customer asked a question. Travis leaned over. "He likes you, Mom. Did you see
the way he looked at you?"

I shook my head.

"Well, pay attention," he said in a slightly annoyed
tone.

I left the store with too many fish, since I lost my con-
centration halfway through the purchase, but I reminded
myself that it was an important learning lesson as I
dumped the remainder of the smelt into the garbage the
following week.

Risk Every Day

If we're alert and unafraid to risk, we'll find all kinds of
opportunities presenting themselves on a regular basis.
I have met men in the following ways:

- On the phone. In an effort to call my ex-husband in
  a neighboring state, I forgot to dial the area code
  and instead got a nice eligible bachelor in a neighboring town. We still talk on the phone three years
  later.
- In the canned-food section of the local grocery store.
- On the shuttle to the airport.
- In the optical store. He sold me my first pair of
  glasses.
- Through my son (his best friend's dad).
- At my twenty-year high school reunion.

With a little energy and a lot of risk taking, our looking
might pay off someday.

If our looking does pay off and we actually still like the
person after a few dates, we need to bring our kids into
the relationship as soon as possible. But, remember—they
want a dad, and kids can be pretty single-minded when
they decide what they want.

It doesn't take much, sometimes.

"Mom, he's cool. He likes pro wrestling."

"Grab him, Mom. He's got a boat."

"Did he say he worked at Nordstrom? Wow! Think of the discounts."

It won't matter to them if he has three heads, as long as each of his heads functions in the role of daddy and meets their particular needs.

Have you ever noticed that when kids want something really bad, they become slightly frantic, and the longer they're put off, the more frantic they become?

We need to prepare ourselves for that. When they're desperate, every man you bring home is daddy material, and they'll have you marching down the aisle before you've memorized the guy's name.

That is, if you're looking. What about if you're not looking? How do you calm the natives then?

When You're Not Lookin'

There is little to say about all this if you're not looking. Then the dilemma is what to do with your kids' hopes of ever being a "regular" family—dad, mom, kids, dog. Is it loving to lead our kids to believe that that is our goal when it's not? Should it be our goal just because our kids have made it their goal?

If everyone is committed to the unit idea, you can level with them about why you're not looking and help them work through their individual disappointments to a place of acceptance.

If they're in the very common self-centered mode and not committed to the unit, it doesn't matter what you do or say; it will never be enough, and it will never be right. Save your energy.

God knows what's best for us. It's important that we

stay open to whatever "best" means for our particular family. Just as there are valid reasons for looking, there are valid reasons for not looking:

- You don't believe in (re)marriage
- A relationship with a man ultimately seems to lead to love, an affair, or marriage, none of which you wish to pursue at this present time, if ever
- You're too busy
- You like being single

Okay. You're not looking. Either way, what do we do with the needs created by the absence of a husband-father figure?

"Mom, my watch is broken."

"Mom, my leg is broken."

"Mom, my heart is broken."

Daddies come in handy for lots of things. They can fix things like watches, and they care about things like broken legs and broken hearts. Well, many do; we have no guarantee.

A family without a husband-father does create a void.

Some broken watches can be repaired; some are never quite the same.

Some broken legs can be fixed; if diseased, some have to be amputated; and some people are suddenly quite unexpectedly paraplegic or quadraplegic. Their bodies are never quite the same.

Some broken hearts heal, yet when a loved one dies or a relationship shatters, a void will always exist. The heart is never quite the same. But God is in the business of redeeming and healing and restoring and mending, and a family without a husband-father may never be the same, but it can be okay with God. It can be more than okay—it can be complete.

How?

God has a way of building His people from the inside out. He is never hindered by physical limitations; He's creative. God has more than one way to accomplish His purposes.

Following are some practical tips in getting your husband-daddy needs met.

Appeal to the Former Male Figure

If the relationship is still a congenial one, don't be too proud to beg. Some men want little or nothing to do with what they've walked away from or been kicked out of. Some former spouses are abusive, and you don't want them near you or your kids. Each situation is different.

But on occasion, everyone stays on friendly terms. If this is your case, let the man continue to provide physical, emotional, and spiritual support. Even if he can provide just one of the three, take it.

Caution: We must help our kids keep their perspective. For a while, my kids wanted to call their father every time I couldn't afford to buy them something.

"Mom, I saw this cool jean jacket at Nordstrom."

"I can't—"

"Afford it? No problem. I'll call Dad."

"Let me talk," another one piped up. "I need a pair of basketball shoes."

Their view of their dad was becoming too one-dimensional.

We don't want to *use* the other person. (Okay, sometimes we do, but when we recognize it, we really should get a grip.)

Take Care of the Need Yourself

Is the need physical? I've assembled a baby crib without written instructions, put up a basketball hoop, and repaired the clutch in my car.

Is the need emotional? Yes, a daddy's arms and shoulder feel different from a mommy's. But if a daddy isn't available, a mommy's will do. Like a daddy, a mommy has two arms to wrap around her children and two ears to listen to her little ones' problems.

Is the need spiritual? Don't buy into the myth that says in order to have a happy Christian home, a daddy must lead family devotions every night. A mommy can lead family devotions, and if family devotions aren't your thing, you can lead whatever is. A spiritual leader is simply a guide who gets and keeps everyone on the path to God.

When the pressure's on, we can do a lot more than we think we can, and if you're a single parent, the pressure's on.

My kids have fixed boom boxes, built elaborate forts, and repaired flat bicycle tires by themselves. They've cried on one another's shoulders at times and encouraged one another in the Lord at other times.

We're all learning not to blame our unmet needs on the absence of a daddy but to take care of things ourselves when we can.

Let God Provide a Father Figure

God has given us a man named Fred. Fred is a math teacher who has tutored my son in math. He has worked on forts with my boys and cuddled in front of the television with my girls. He's taken my kids to ball games and calls frequently just to check on us.

Sometimes we are so into our own pain that we miss

God's provision. And sometimes we're too proud to admit that we need help.

Father figures aren't particularly easy to find; most men are too caught up with their own families to have much time for anyone else. Because of that, they may not be sensitive to needs around them unless they're pointed out. If we can get past our pride and make our needs known, God may put it on someone's heart to respond.

To be honest, though, for whatever reasons, He may not. Or maybe no one is available.

Let God Help You Cope With Unmet Needs

The sad reality of life is that all our needs may not be met in the way we think they should be.

The Apostle Paul said he knew what it was to be in need and also what it was to have everything he wanted. He had learned contentment in all situations. He went on to say that "God will meet all your needs according to his glorious riches in Christ Jesus" (Philippians 4:19).

The question is, what are our needs? God may view the whole thing differently than we do. "His glorious riches in Christ Jesus" may be other than the meat and potatoes we're used to. I don't know that God views life in the tangible way we do.

Looking or not, the more I know God, the more I know that He is close, taking care of our family in the best and only way that He can. He loves us.

"Mom, are you lookin'? Have you found anything yet?"

"Not yet, Grant. You'll be the first to know if and when I do."

In the meantime, we can pray with our kids: "Though my father and [or] mother forsake me, the Lord will receive me" (Psalm 27:10).

4
WHAT DO YOU MEAN HE'S A GEEK?

Getting Their Approval

"Oh, Mom, you're not wearing that, are you?"

"Mom, where did you meet that dude you went out with last night? What planet is he from?"

"Mom, you're kidding, right? You're not really thinking about buying that ugly yellow car we looked at yesterday?"

As single moms, we have no other adult in the immediate vicinity to validate our personal choices and decisions. We're at the mercy of our kids' opinions. On a secure day, we may sail through with only a few bumps and scratches. If our kids aren't presently working toward a united front, put-down after put-down may shake our confidence in our ability to make the best choices.

How important is a child's approval? Does it suddenly become more important when we've lost a mate? Do we allow our kids' opinions to sway us? Do we always need to take them into consideration when making decisions?

Where do we draw the line between holding onto our own opinions and letting our kids dictate our every move?

These are important questions. If we can answer them honestly, we'll perceive definite clues as to why we might have some relationship problems in our unit.

The desire for our kids' approval is normal, especially for single parents. However, a desperate need for it because of insecurity is not healthy.

A parent's need for approval is often unconscious and reveals itself in subtle ways. A single father's struggle for his children's approval is usually expressed differently from a single mother's. Under pressure we may revert to certain kinds of stereotyped male/female force. A father may work to get approval by forcing his kids to believe as he does. He accomplishes this through his own forms of disapproval of his kids. A single mother, on the other hand, may use manipulation to get her kids' approval.

Since the desire for approval is a normal need, but the demand for it is not a healthy expression, how do we tell the difference, and how can we keep this desire in perspective when we don't have a mate with whom to share these dilemmas?

Desire and Desperate Need

When the phone rang, I stumbled over various book bags and toys to answer it, but Dwight had already picked it up and was now saying to me, "It's that geek, Todd," not bothering to cover the mouthpiece, of course.

Throwing him a murderous glance, I wrenched the receiver from his hand. "Hi, Todd," I said sweetly.

Later, when I finally caught up with and cornered my son, I demanded, "How could you say such a thing? He could hear you!"

"I was two feet away," he defended himself. "Besides, he *is* a geek. He probably already knows it. Geeks know who they are."

"Even if they do, I'm sure they'd rather not have other people point it out."

He shrugged, smiled, and walked away.

No matter how nicely Todd treated my kids, no matter how positively I talked about him, they continued to call him a geek, make faces when he called, and mutter private jokes to one another that resulted in gales of laughter whenever his name came up.

They refused to give in. I might as well have been dating Pee-Wee Herman. They simply had no respect for the guy. Naturally, I took it personally. I had, after all, *chosen* to date Todd.

I want my kids to like the guys I date. I want them to like my clothes. I also want their approval of:

- The food I put on the table
- My salary. I want them to think that I make at least as much as their friends' parents
- My intelligence
- My beliefs. I want them to think that I'm a progressive thinker
- My friends

And the list goes on. Hardly a day goes by that I don't at some point think, *I want you guys to like this. How can I present this idea (or person) so that you'll like it?*

What I'm really saying is . . . *so that you'll like me.* That is where the list ends—with me. I want their approval of me.

Is my desire for approval a desperate need? Sometimes. I'm learning to discern between a simple desire for their approval and a desperate need for it.

My son enters the room, hears the song playing on the radio, and exclaims, "What is that?" Laughter. "Mom, what are you listening to?"

Until that point, I've hummed along with the song. I like the song; it might even be one of my favorites. Yet when my son appears, I react in one of three ways:

- "What song?" I pretend to listen. "Oh, you must mean that one on the radio." I laugh. "I don't know what station that is. I just turned it on." If I didn't like the song, this would be a perfectly normal response.
- "My favorite song. I love it. If you don't like it, you can leave and come back when it's over." I smile sweetly.
- "Never mind what I'm listening to. What do you care, anyway? Don't think you can tell me what music to listen to. It's a lot better than that heavy metal junk you like."

If I react in the last way, I'm in the danger zone. Stop. Think. What would elicit such an angry reaction?

Why do we need their approval? Was that the question? Their approval is not so much an issue when we know we have it. It only becomes an issue when it's withheld.

Our kids' lack of approval says an awful lot about us parents. Even if we know, rationally, that we're doing okay, a child's disapproving frown challenges our confidence.

We can't always please our kids or anyone else, so what did Paul mean when he said, "Each of us should please his neighbor for his good, to build him up" (Romans 15:2)? If our neighbors are those God places closest in our lives, then our kids must fall into that category.

Paul goes on to talk about "the God who gives endurance and encouragement" giving us "a spirit of unity" among ourselves (Romans 15:5). He concludes with an admonition to "accept one another, then, just as Christ accepted you" (Romans 15:7).

I interpret all this to mean pretty much what I've said all along: The goal is to get each child to function as part of the whole unit. Yes, we would love to please them. It would be wonderful if all our choices and decisions made our children ecstatic. But if we could always please them, why would we need to worry about endurance, encouragement, unity, and acceptance, as the above Scripture exhorts?

God understands kids; He was one once.

Travis eyed me critically. "Mom, stonewashed jeans aren't in anymore." He shook his head sadly.

I looked down at my jeans in horror. "Not in? I paid fifty-four dollars for these jeans. How do you know they're not in? I can't believe it." I glared at him, holding him fully responsible for the fashion trends in our country. "I have no intention of throwing these perfectly good jeans out just because they're not in."

"Suit yourself." He shook his head again and clucked his tongue. "Just thought you'd like to know." Smiling, he walked away, knowing full well that I'd throw the jeans out because they weren't "in." Some things are important to me, and my kids know what they are. Being "in" is one of them.

Actually, after much deliberation, to both Travis's and my surprise, I decided to keep the jeans. Sometimes when one weighs all the factors, one must make an alternate decision based on current data. Were other data to have surfaced, one might have made a different decision.

Travis's disapproval was definitely an important factor, as was walking around in outdated jeans. But the fifty-four dollars was also a factor. Besides, I liked the jeans; they were comfortable.

This little incident revealed to me that I was not in a danger zone; I desired Travis's approval but didn't desperately need it.

To me, pleasing my neighbor (kid) means considering that person when making decisions concerning that person. My kids will ride in the car and live in the house. Therefore I want their input on the family vehicle and the house and neighborhood in which we live. As an individual and as part of the unit, each child's input matters.

Of course, just because I open up something for discussion doesn't mean I'm automatically going to act on the input. It does mean I will give it serious consideration.

Kids know when their input means more than it should. The times kids can most easily manipulate me are the times I'm in the most desperate need of their approval.

"Mom, when we stayed at Beth's last week while you were on that trip, she made all these fancy dinners, and we had dessert every night."

I stared at the runny macaroni and cheese on our plates. It didn't get much better than this, either.

"Mom, Jennifer's mom gives her a ride to school every single day." Sigh. "She must really care about her daughter."

Three blocks; it's only three blocks. Am I neglecting my child, who has to walk three blocks to school, rain or shine? Who knows for sure?

Why do I feel so bad? I want my kids to think I'm great, the best parent in the world. I remember a mother of seven whose children fought regularly over who would get to sit next to her at dinner. At our house, I barely finish cooking dinner before my kids are scraping it out of the pan and running downstairs to the family room so they don't miss one precious moment of some TV program.

If your kids don't approve of you or your decisions, does that mean you're a bad parent? Is that why the desire for approval turns into a desperate need?

The way our kids view us is not always the determining factor in gauging how well we're doing as parents. Their opinions can be purely subjective.

One son says, "Mom, I hate it when you go out. Stay home with us." The voice of insecurity.

Another son says, "Mom, you need to go out more—meet some guys." The voice of security.

How do you keep the desire for your kids' approval from turning into a desperate need?

- Give yourself a break. Quit trying so hard. You're doing the best you can.
- Give yourself permission to be imperfect.
- Face reality. Your kids are going to disapprove of you and your actions sometimes. You'll live.
- Fully realize that your kids' opinions are not the final say on your worth and value, either as a parent or as a person.
- Your identity as a person is found in your relationship with God, not in your role as a parent.

Position and Age

A child's age and position in the family have a lot to do with how I process the input and how much I need the approval.

Jesus was twelve when Mary found Him in the temple

courts sitting with the teachers, listening and asking questions. He'd been missing for three days. When confronted with His confusing behavior, He simply answered, "Why were you searching for me? Didn't you know I had to be in my Father's house?" (*See* Luke 2:41–51.)

I wonder what Mary thought. She knew full well that she had given birth to the Son of God. When their schedules or lives were at cross-purposes, hers in her humanness and His in His divinity, I wonder if she ever questioned her ability to mother this God-child. I wonder if, as He "grew in wisdom and stature, and in favor with God and men" (Luke 2:52), Mary ever desperately needed her son's approval. He was, after all, God.

No, Mary had no edge on Jesus when it came to understanding the purpose of life.

My kids think they know it all. They would like me to believe that the vast knowledge and experience they have acquired in their ten to fifteen years on the planet has equipped them to handle life in the fast lane or any lane they choose.

For instance, Travis is obsessed with Donald Trump. Everything I know about this tycoon I've learned from my son.

I have a daughter who knows more about sex at age ten than I knew at thirty. "Mom, if you have sex one hour and then do it again the next hour, you get twins."

Okay, she does have some misconceptions, but I'm sure she could teach me a lot.

This would all be extremely intimidating if I desperately needed my kids' approval.

I'm finding that their position in the family, as well as their age, makes a huge difference as to how seriously I take and how much I need their input and approval.

When my oldest son went to live with his father, suddenly my second son, Dwight, was thrust into the position of oldest. Whereas before he'd acted more like a child, always making room for his older brother, now he began expressing some opinions of his own. I listened; his opinions carried more weight than before. I found myself needing his approval much more than when he'd been so passive.

"Mom, the black pants look better with that shirt."

"Thanks, Dwight."

Transcending Disapproval

As we've already established, our kids will sometimes disapprove of us. Some of our kids will usually disapprove of us.

How do we handle that?

Love, approval, acceptance—we need these things from our kids, just as they need them from us. These are the unit's human needs, nothing to be ashamed of.

All my kids, at one time or another, have disapproved of me because of the divorce. They have blamed me. Like the persistent widow in Jesus' parable (Luke 18:2–8), my heart cried out for justice.

But at times, instead of justice, the walls between my kids and myself seemed higher than ever, certainly too high to scale. They didn't or couldn't understand. Too young, they could only react out of their own pain.

Now, some years later, justice is finally mine. One by one, they have come to a place of understanding.

How did I survive the years of being misunderstood? How did I face their disapproval? I know one thing: If I had accepted the blame, if I had taken on their accusations

and beat up on myself, justice would have eluded me.
Likewise, if I had fiercely defended myself, blaming their
father for all of the problems in the marriage, I doubt if
their respect would have ever returned.

". . . their thoughts now accusing, now even defending
them. . . . Each one should be fully convinced in his own
mind" (Romans 2:15, 14:5).

Unless we succumb to our kids' every demand, disapproval can't be avoided. How do we transcend it?

- Live your life. When the disapproving frowns,
  rolled eyeballs, and sneers come at you, hold
  steady. Encourage yourself with: "It is the Lord [not
  my kids] who judges me" (1 Corinthians 4:4). Justice is on its way.
- Teach your kids to express their disapproval in an
  acceptable way. Acceptable: "Mom, I disagree with
  what you're saying (doing, wearing, planning), but
  I fight for your right to say (do, wear, plan) it."
  Unacceptable: frowns, rolled eyeballs, sneers, ridicule, mouthing off, and so forth.
- Remind the kids that there's a head of the house
  and, like it or not, you're it. You appreciate their
  input when it's presented in an acceptable way,
  but after you evaluate it, *you* will make the final
  decision.

"Mom, why would you want to date a geek, anyway?"
"For your information, his geekiness has not been
established," I returned confidently. "That is only your
opinion."
"Oh yeah?"
"Yeah."
Once we understand where disapproval comes from, it

is more easily transcended. Most often, when our kids, for whatever surface reason, disapprove of us, they are:

- Insecure
- Afraid
- Embarrassed

If we can hold steady and not panic, we can ride the waves of our kids' disapproval. Our unit can stay afloat. It cannot only stay afloat but it can sail.

Jesus rode the waves a lot. The Pharisees were forever disapproving of and judging His actions, words, and motives. His answer to them? "Before Abraham was born, I am" (John 8:58). He knew who He was. So must we.

5
BUT I NEVER CLAIMED TO BE PERFECT

Teaching Your Kids Values When They Catch You Sinning

"I can't believe we're doing this," I whispered to my friend Patti as I boosted myself up to the sill and climbed out my open bedroom window and onto the roof of my house. I turned to help Patti, who, not as agile as I was (Agile? well, my agility certainly didn't come from doing this regularly!), moaned and groaned as she slid over the ledge and through the open window on her stomach.

"Ooomph!" She thumped her way onto the roof like a seal out of water.

"Ssh!" I hissed. We held perfectly still and quiet, hoping my kids hadn't picked up the peculiar noises from the roof.

Assured that we were safe, Patti, clutching the shingles, crawled gingerly over to me and crouched beside me, where she exhaled deeply.

"I really can't believe it," I muttered. "I'm thirty-eight years old, sitting on my roof in the black of night, freezing to death."

Patti started to giggle, but the roof was slanted and her rocking laughter caused her to lose her balance. She started to slide down the roof, but I caught her. Sobering, she peered over the edge.

"It's a ways down there," she said as she crept slowly back to my side. She then pulled out of her pocket the reason for our excursion onto the roof: a pack of cigarettes. She lit one, inhaled, then exhaled. "Aaah," she sighed in relief. "It was all worth it."

"For you, maybe. What am I getting out of the deal?"

"The pleasure of my company," she returned smugly.

"This is crazy. I mean, kids are the ones who climb out the window when they want to smoke, not adults. I feel like I'm back in junior high. If you weren't so afraid of my kids—"

"I have every right to be afraid of your kids," Patti said. "You heard how Grant was talking about smokers yesterday. They're all sinners and headed for the hot place. And the look on Merilee's face the other day when we passed that girl smoking. She looked so sad, like she'd just witnessed a tragic accident."

"That's their problem," I said in an effort to calm Patti's anxiety. "You can't—"

The bedroom door that I had so carefully locked (I thought) suddenly flew open and three of my five kids burst into the room. Beside me, Patti choked on her cigarette. "I thought you locked the door," she hissed.

Spotting the open window, they charged across the room, where they caught Patti exhaling the last puff of the cigarette she'd frantically tossed over the edge (probably onto the roof of my van).

"I did," I hissed back as I smiled through gritted teeth at

the three faces peering out into the darkness at their mother and her friend on the roof.

They smelled it. "You're smoking," Grant accused.

I looked sheepish. "Not me, Grant. You know I don't smoke."

Patti groaned and tried to hide behind me. I knew she was bracing herself for Grant's lecture.

But he grinned. "Why are you on the roof?" He laughed. Now that they knew it wasn't their mother who was smoking, they could see the funny side. They all began to laugh.

We couldn't help it; Patti and I started giggling. We were caught, shamed by my kids for sneaking a smoke. Might as well laugh at life today and worry tomorrow about how I would phrase my next parental lecture on why smoking is hazardous to your health.

It's true that I wasn't the one caught smoking. There was some consolation in that. However, as a mother, I had for a period of time indulged in the habit and tried to hide it from my kids. I wouldn't blame them if they didn't trust me not to do that again.

When Patti was gone, I knew I'd have an honest discussion with my kids and that they'd have some questions. We did and they did. I assured them that no, I really hadn't taken up smoking again, and I didn't believe Patti's final destination was the "hot place" because she smoked.

Did I feel like a hypocrite because I taught my kids the evils of smoking and then played a major part as an accomplice in supporting my smoking friend's habit by hiding her from her would-be accusers?

Because I'm a parent struggling to teach my kids, both in word and by example, to develop honest and loving patterns of relating to God and others, does that mean I have to be perfect? Am I not allowed mistakes? Does that mean in my humanness I won't ever sin?

Or does it mean that I can acknowledge my sins to God and myself, oftentimes to my kids, and appropriate God's forgiveness?

What happens in a divorced home where one parent teaches the kids one set of values and the other parent teaches them another? What's to prevent mass confusion? I'm sure that one reason smoking is such an issue with my kids is that it's an issue with their father. I don't get uptight about smoking. Obviously, or I wouldn't have been out on the roof.

Yet I do have my uptight areas. I feel strongly about:

- Loyalty
- Justice
- Integrity
- Individual freedom

My kids have their uptight areas. They feel strongly about:

- Personal rights
- Personal space
- Personal curfews
- Batman

So you can see how there might be a conflict of interests in the family. Does everyone in the family have to agree on values in order for the family to function healthily?

It would certainly make things easier. But to be realistic, I'm not sure agreeing on values is always an attainable goal or should even be the desired goal.

Values evolve from a belief system constructed mostly in childhood. Since parents cannot be with their children every moment of every day (I personally do not mind that), a child's peers, teachers, and television heroes contribute to the constructing of his or her belief system.

Beliefs

Travis was about nine when I first realized that my child had a mind of his own—a thinking mind, even. A mind that wondered, rationalized, solved problems, and sometimes even arrived at conclusions different from mine.

"Mom, just because you believe in God, does that mean I have to?" he asked as we drove down the street one day to soccer practice.

My heart raced and my car veered into the oncoming lane. Amazingly enough, I regained control before we collided head-on with a station wagon.

My mind tore off in a number of directions.

Of course you do, was my first thought. *You always have to believe the way I do. Because I've lived for thirty-some years, I'm wise, and I know what's best for you.*

What do you mean? was my next panicky thought. *Why would you even ask that? Are you thinking about not believing in Him? What are they teaching you at that horrible atheistic school?*

That's a silly question—thought number three. *Let's talk about it when you're twenty-one.*

Oh, no, I'm losing my son! Last irrational response. *This is so depressing. We'll no longer be able to share this huge area of our lives—the spiritual. This is so sad.*

"Mom? Do I?" he asked patiently.

"God, You're on," I muttered.

"What, Mom?"

"Oh, well. I—no, actually God wants us to choose to believe in Him because we want to, because we love Him, not because someone else believes in Him or tells us to."

Even if that someone is your mother. I sighed.

"Really? Oh, wow." He looked too pleased.

My heart ceased its racing and seemed to stop altogether.

"I do, of course—you know—believe in Him. I was just wondering."

What a risk, freeing my child to choose his own beliefs, for that is exactly what my words did for him. I could have taken advantage of his nine-year-old innocence and imposed my belief system on him. "Yes, you do have to believe in God, because I said so." Compliant child that he was, he would have accepted that for a while. But because of his questioning mind and his active imagination, my belief system would have become a prison. His goal would have been to find a way of escape.

But God came through. Instead of imprisoning him, my words freed him to believe in God or not believe in Him. Now, years later, he is still free and still exploring, although more intensely. Yes, he's still asking uncomfortable questions, and sometimes his search takes him into dangerous territory.

But I know—I can't explain how—I just know that God has His hand on Travis's life. Travis is an earnest seeker after truth, and the truth is what set Travis free when he was nine, just as it sets him free today. Since Jesus Christ is the truth (John 14:6), I know where my son's search is leading him.

Surprisingly, since Travis's provocative question, I have learned that all my children have minds that think and question and wonder. It definitely keeps me on my toes.

Sometimes I wonder if I'm doing this right. Am I giving them more freedom than they can handle? Do you ever wonder about that? We are the parents, after all. Don't we have the right to tell our kids what to believe so the family will be unified?

I think not. I have learned through experience, as well as by watching others, that a relationship with God that is built on love is the only kind that's honest, the only kind that satisfies our souls. And it can only be honest when it's *ours*. Children need to be free to experience and enjoy their own relationship with their own personal God, not their parents' version of God.

That's the risky part. What if they choose to believe in a God that looks quite different from ours? Will God hold us responsible for that? Does that mean we failed as parents?

In the Great Commission, if it can be applied here, Jesus told us single parents to teach our kids to obey everything He commanded us. He didn't add, "And if they don't, it's your fault." No, His next words were, "And surely I am with you always" (Matthew 28:20). He will be with us no matter what our kids do with our teaching.

So I teach my kids one set of values, their father teaches them another, the school teaches them something else. I believe they're going to listen to those with whom they have the most honest and loving relationships, so I focus on teaching my values in as honest and loving a way as I can. The truth is, my belief system is not flawless. I tell them that. I don't know all the answers. "But this is how I see it. You may see it a different way. Let's love each other no matter what."

As we all know, our beliefs determine our behavior. I may say I believe one thing, yet my actions may reveal the opposite. What's to keep the family stable?

Behavior

"Mom, how come you tell us we can't eat in the front room and you sit here eating ice cream?"

"Mom, don't talk to me about my horrible temper. You totally maxed out with Amber today. I saw you."

I teach my kids honesty. Yet sometimes I:

- Elaborate on the truth
- Cover up the truth
- Deny the truth

I teach my kids loyalty. Yet sometimes I:

- Gossip
- Fail to let my love cover another's sin
- Carelessly reveal another's weakness
- Stay quiet when love says defend

I teach my kids to always give others the freedom to choose. Yet sometimes I:

- Try to control others
- Manipulate others to get what I want
- Fearfully clutch when I need to let go
- Make choices for others out of an unhealthy sense of responsibility

Our behavior cannot be separated from our belief system; our belief system determines our behavior. When our behavior is inconsistent with what we claim to believe, it is often because the belief is only in our head and hasn't yet worked its way into our heart. This is where our kids come in handy. They are quick to spot hypocrisy or inconsistencies in our lives, and they are quick to tell us when they do—whether or not we ask.

Since our kids are in the process of forming beliefs, much, if not most, of their behavior is determined by their feelings. Our responsibility is to teach our kids how to deal with their feelings so their emotions do not drive them to ungodly behavior and so their belief system is formed not by feelings but by the Bible.

How does that happen when we are so imperfect? Is it even possible for one person to keep the unit on track? I've noticed that marriage seems to keep people accountable. A married couple have each other to answer to. They decide together the code of ethics or values by which the unit will abide. At least, that's the ideal; I realize many marriages fall short of the ideal.

But single parents don't have that option. Alone, we struggle through life and teach our kids our values, either by word or action. We hope they pick up the good while God redeems our inconsistencies.

In the meantime, what do we do with the kids who demand perfection from their imperfect and very human parents?

Honesty

We have one value in our family that underlies all the rest and that I refuse to sacrifice: the value of honesty. No matter where the unit falls down, we come back to honesty.

I have chosen to believe in my kids and to believe that unless proven otherwise, they relate truthfully to me and I to them. Sometimes it all backfires, and we have to start over. Still, we can only start over if we're committed to honesty in the unit. I refuse to even attempt to address, let alone try to resolve, a problem without it.

For example, we have a commitment (I prefer the word *commitment* to rule) to avoid the use of profanity in our family. Yet on occasion, a crude word (one on our black-list) slips out of my mouth before I can catch it. This always evokes a discussion on the subject.

"Mom, can I say _____ when I'm with my friends?" Merilee asked. "They all say _____. I'm the only one who can't."

My answer to this question? "Actually, I don't like the idea of your saying _____ with your friends. *Why did she have to ask, anyway?* It sounds unfeminine or something. I mean, it's crude."

She stared at me blankly. Could I blame her? When I was ten years old, was I worried about being crude? "But they all say it," she whined. "I'm the only one. . . ."

Yes, that's what I worried about at the age of ten—being the only one who couldn't do something. That was the real issue, not _____. So we talked about that, and I really don't know what she decided to do about saying _____.

Then one day seven-year-old Amber said, "Mom, do people go to hell for saying bad words?"

"People go to hell for refusing to accept Jesus' death on the cross and forgiveness of their sins, not for saying bad words." I was about to break that answer down into terms she could understand, but my answer had satisfied her. She nodded and ran off to play.

I should have known she had a reason for asking. I discovered a few days later that what she had really meant was whether *she* would go to hell for saying bad words, for suddenly the neighbors were reporting to me regularly, and they weren't happy.

"I don't appreciate the word Amber taught Rachel."

"Are you aware of the words Amber has been using lately?"

"Where has Amber been hanging out these days? The local tavern?"

Needless to say, we had another honest talk.

"But Mom, you said I wouldn't go to hell."

Should I have told Amber that people went to hell for saying bad words in order to control her mouth? It would have worked, and I would have saved myself much embarrassment.

No, because it's not the truth. I let God redeem it by taking the opportunity to establish fresh guidelines for behavior based on love for God and others, not punishment.

Right now, things are quiet in this area, but I predict that someone will say a bad word somewhere up the line and we will do this all over again.

We must remember that the goal of the unit is not perfect behavior. The goal is to learn how to relate honestly and lovingly to others within and without the unit.

To me, a big part of relating honestly and lovingly is to fully acknowledge, rather than repress, my sinful tendencies or weaknesses—when God requires it.

I came home one day to the smell of marijuana. I followed the sickly sweet smell to my son's bedroom.

"I can't believe it!" I shrieked. "You're smoking dope—right in our house!" Did he think I was born yesterday, that I wouldn't recognize the smell of marijuana? What did he take me for? I was appalled that he would be so bold as to smoke dope in our home.

However, my next feeling appalled me even more. Committed to honesty, I had to acknowledge it, at least to myself: I was tempted. A nice Christian thirty-eight-year-old mother like myself!

My reaction shouldn't have surprised me. I was, after all, a child of the pot-smoking sixties generation. I indulged fairly regularly during my teen years. After all these years, the smell of marijuana took me back to my youth.

My son stood there, petrified, waiting for the ax to fall, and I was lost somewhere in the past. I returned to the present and stared at my son. He was a mere child, really, experimenting with dope. I understood, and I knew he would listen to me only if he knew I understood.

Honesty. God was requiring it.

"Honey, I want to tell you something. When I was your age. . . ."

That was a year ago. We talked about it the other day. He told me he has never smoked pot since that night. I choose to believe him, for we have a commitment to honesty in our family.

Some parents would disagree with our kind of honesty. How can I maintain my parental authority if my kids discover that I've done everything I'm telling them not to?

The truth is, I have not earned my right to parent because of perfect behavior. God has given me five precious gifts to train and teach—honestly and lovingly.

My son has never once thrown my past back into my face, using it as an excuse to do his own thing. He might have. I took a risk. Another time, with another child, I might not have admitted that particular weakness. A commitment to honesty doesn't mean I spill all my guts to all my kids all the time about everything. Absolutely not.

What it does mean is that I don't try to pretend I am anything other than human, just as they are. That is what

God requires: that we be who we are, very human single parents doing the best we can to raise our kids to love God, others, and themselves.

Love—The Highest Value

Jesus made it plain to His disciples: " 'Love the Lord' . . . . This is the first and greatest commandment. And the second is like it: 'Love your neighbor as yourself' " (Matthew 22:37–39).

Love is the reason we exist, our purpose for being, our highest value. If I teach my kids nothing else, I hope I teach them something about loving.

Yet here we go again. As single parents, we teach our kids to be lovers, but we ourselves love so imperfectly. One reason is just that: We are *single* parents. Our own need to be loved is so great at times.

I once heard a speaker say, "When you first meet someone, you will see flash in that person's eyes the question, 'Do you love me?' " It's true. But it's not only when you first meet someone. It's also when you get to know someone. It's the question we all ask during each and every significant encounter with others.

In various ways, my kids ask it daily, and I ask it of them. Above all else that happens in the unit, we must love one another.

How?

- By doing everything right?
- By always behaving sweetly, kindly, and wonderfully?
- By avoiding conflict and confrontation?
- By denying negative feelings?
- By running around meeting everyone's needs?

What do you think? Here are some suggestions that are more realistic than the previous ones and definitely more honest:

- Create a safe atmosphere that enables members of the family to express honest feelings that always keep the channels of love open.
- Hit problems head-on before someone is driven to lie or is embittered and locked into an unloving attitude.
- Use one value to measure all internal attitudes and external behaviors: love.
- Ask not the question, "Is it right?" suggesting a rule, but "Is it loving?" suggesting a character trait.
- Express love.

A mother in her fifties told me recently that she couldn't say "I love you" to her grown children. They hadn't expressed love verbally in their home as the children were growing up, and she couldn't express it now. How tragic.

"Mom, do you love me?" expressed in a look, an action, a word.

"I love you." Three little words, the impact of which is life-changing.

But sometimes we love and love and love some more and it's never enough. Just how responsible are we to make our kids happy and well adjusted in their sojourn toward maturity? (You mean there's an end to all this?)

6
YOU'RE STILL NOT HAPPY?

When All You've Got Isn't Enough

"I am bored. B-O-R-D. I've never been so bored. What a boring, boring day. What a boring life. I never have anything to do."

Oh, dear, I panic, *this poor kid has nothing to do. If I don't think of something fast, he'll be stealing cars or dealing drugs by the time he's ten.*

On another day: "If you and Dad hadn't gotten divorced, you know, I'd have a car right now. We'd have two incomes. We are so-o poor."

Oh, dear, I panic, *it's all my fault. This poor kid is so deprived. I've ruined his life. How can he face his friends each day—carless? This is terrible.*

I'm getting used to the panicky feeling, the feeling that blasts out, "You are responsible for making this child happy—*now.*"

But what if I can't? What if I don't have what it takes? What if a member of the family ultimately turns out to be a miserable adult, contributing nothing to society? Who's to blame? I can hardly blame their father; he lives in another state. I will have failed at the most important calling God's given me.

True? Is it my *most important* calling? Who can measure one calling against another? Am I really a failure if one kid, who happens to be related to me, grows up to be a miserable adult?

Who's Responsible?

It's amazing how early our kids start trying to manipulate us. I remember one particular time soon after my divorce. But it didn't work. I was so exhausted from the emotional stress that I was determined no one would put one more thing on me.

Three-year-old Amber stood, her hands on her hips, and pointed a chubby little index finger at me. "You make me so unhappy," she accused.

"Oh, no, I don't," I returned without hesitation. "You make yourself unhappy, and don't you ever forget it."

She looked confused. This was obviously a brand-new thought. Maybe she got the message; she's never said that since. The other members of the unit have—plenty of times in a variety of ways.

Are our kids responsible for their own happiness? What a load we could lift off ourselves if they are.

I do not believe we are responsible for keeping the unit in a state of blissful happiness, scrambling to "fix" and "prop up" any member whose smile starts to slip. That's called co-dependency, and we are all in the process of being healed from that, right? At the other extreme, I can't just leave my kids to themselves. I do care about their needs and happiness.

The biblical guideline is to "carry each other's burdens . . ." (Galatians 6:2) and also "each one should carry his own load" (Galatians 6:5). That's clear to me. Each member of the family cares about the others but also knows he or she is responsible for his or her personal needs, as well.

We've read all the reams of written material on dysfunctional behavior in families. One goal of a dysfunctional family is for each member to make all the other members feel responsible for his or her pain or happiness. They do this in various ways:

- Shaming
- Manipulating
- Blaming

Our kids instinctively know how to use these techniques. They learn them at birth, for new fathers and mothers fall all over themselves to make and keep their precious little children happy and contented. This goes from the first bottle or breast to the cherry red sports car in the driveway.

We single parents easily fall into the "I'm responsible" trap because we feel "the poor darlings have already suffered so much, I don't want to add to their suffering." However, by taking responsibility for their happiness, we enable them to stay immature and thereby retard the growing-up process.

Enabling

When we hear the word *enabling* we immediately connect it to an alcoholic, workaholic, or drug addict—loved ones who have addiction problems. I wonder if addicts become addicts because they were enabled as children.

Maybe they never learned how to deal with problems in their lives.

You are enabling when:

- Your son decides to cut school or skip work and you write his excuse or call his employer for him
- Your three-year-old cries for her bottle every night and you run to get it because you know she'll hate you if you don't
- You let your oldest child control the home and the other kids with his demands because "it's just so much easier" and you hate confrontation
- You give into your daughter's demands because you know if you don't you'll have to listen to her cry in her room for an hour (or if she's a different kind of child, you'll have to endure her silent treatment)

As single parents, we may fall into enabling patterns because we so desperately need our kids to like us. Our happiness unhealthily depends on our kids' happiness. In times of unhappiness, each member of the family becomes too aware of loneliness and depends on the other members to meet his or her need. But instead of saying, "I'm lonely. I need you," we enable each other in unhealthy ways. Instead of developing the relationship, we begin to lose respect for ourselves and the one we enable and begin to view both ourselves and the other person with contempt. We have refused to deal with a situation honestly and have chosen the path of least resistance.

A huge case of enabling began to occur when my oldest son moved back home. I was so thrilled to have him back, I refused to make any waves—about anything.

Travis took over the bathroom. He simply bellowed

"Get out!" in the morning, and my girls scampered for cover.

He needed to be at school earlier, I reasoned. I let it go.

He took over the refrigerator and ate *all* of everything. "Travis ate four packages of Pop-Tarts," Merilee wailed one day. "Amber and I only got one each." Travis's logic? "I'm a growing young man. I should have the majority of the food. I'm twice as big as the girls. I should have at least twice as much."

It made sense, so I let it go.

He entered the girls' bedroom anytime he felt like it and sprawled his lanky frame all over Merilee's daybed to watch television.

"My bed's too short for me," he explained.

This was true; I'd have to get him a different bed. I let it go.

When I finally woke up to what I was doing, it was almost too late. He was everywhere. He was used to being everywhere. He liked being everywhere. In order for us to stop enabling him, we had to let him express unhappiness with us. We had to watch him roll his eyes, pull away from us sometimes, think we were stupid.

We hung in, though. Eventually, we claimed our space back. Everyone is entitled to his or her own space.

If you are feeling controlled by one or all of your kids, if you have moments of resentment because of it, you could be enabling. If so, you can do something about it.

To stop enabling:

- Refuse to take responsibility for your child's happiness (or unhappiness), no matter how many times you hear "If you would just. . . ." "You don't care about me. . . ." or "It's your fault I'm. . . ."

- Refuse to "caretake" (or smother) your child, no matter how often you're confronted with soulful, angry, or pleading looks.
- Train your child to take responsibility for his or her decisions and feelings, no matter how often you are made to feel responsible for yours and theirs . . . and the dog's.

The most difficult part of letting go of our enabling patterns of relating to our kids is that we have to watch them hurt. We have to let them be unhappy and purposely not rescue them from their pain.

Letting Them Hurt

"OUCH!"

"Ouch. . . ."

"Ouch?"

Over the years, I have listened to many people scream and cry and whisper "ouch." It always hurts me to hear it. For a mother, is there any "ouch" quite like her child's? It's a distinct "ouch" that sets itself apart from all other ouches and pulls at the strings of her heart. It is one thing to watch and hear; it is quite another to know she has contributed to the plaintive cry.

Pain is a reality. We are doing our kids a terrible disservice if we try to protect them from it. Better they learn about pain while they're still under our wing than when they're thrust out into the dark, cruel world alone. The Holy Spirit is our Comforter; we can teach our kids about Him. Jesus is our Healer; we can teach our kids about His healing power. God is our Father; without pain, our kids will never feel the need to crawl up into His lap. Pain drives us to relationship with God, and our kids follow our example. If they watch us, as adults, expend every available ounce of energy to avoid pain, they will do the same.

Sometimes we can only learn what God wants to teach us through pain.

It was a wet, drizzly Sunday afternoon. Grant, the bored one, had moved from boredom to misery.

"No wonder I'm bored," he complained. "We're so poor. We don't even have a VCR or a computer or anything. If you were married, we'd at least have some money—"

Grant's voice droned on. I stared at the bewhiskered faces in the newspaper in an article on the homeless. I'd read a dozen stories like the one accompanying this photo, so why did something suddenly stir inside me now?

"*Everyone* has more money than we do. Maybe you could get a different job. Or maybe you could get another one besides—"

The stirring wouldn't leave. I had to show him. He had to see it for himself. "Grant, get in the car."

"Huh?"

"Get in the car."

He obeyed, assuming, I'm sure, that I had given in at last. We must be on the way to buy a VCR or something else to entertain him.

"Where are we going?" he asked.

"You'll see. I just want you to keep your eyes and ears open."

When the tall Seattle skyscrapers came into view, Grant realized we weren't going all the way downtown just to buy a new toy.

"I want to show you something," I answered his hundredth "Where are we going?"

Finally at my destination, I drove slowly past the men and women slouched in doorways, sprawled on sidewalks, drinking and playing cards on park benches. Past the food line that snaked around the corner and up two blocks: men, women, and children waiting to appease their hunger.

"Wanna get out and take a walk?" I asked.

He shook his head.

We stopped at a light and one man chased another around our van. The one in pursuit clutched a knife. (*God, I want Grant to get the message, but does it have to be quite this graphic?*)

When I spotted a group of people in the park singing and serving hot dogs to the homeless, I figured it was safe to get out. I parked the car and we began to walk. The smell of urine assaulted our senses as we stepped over a young man lying in his vomit and tried not to wonder if he was dead or alive.

Grant tucked his hand in mine.

"Spare change?" an old guy stared at us with bloodshot eyes.

"I want to give him my money, Mom. I got fifty cents."

I nodded.

He was beginning to get it, but it was on the way home that he finally broke. "Mom, I can feel it coming."

"What?"

"The heartbrokenness." And he cried.

That night as I tucked him into bed, his eyes grew moist once again. "We can't feed them all," he groaned.

"No, we can't."

Neither could we avert our eyes and hearts and not feel their pain. Ever since that day, Grant's life goal has been to someday have a house with a huge backyard, so he can build a bunch of shanties to house all the homeless he plans to collect.

Grant heard and felt some ouches on Skid Row that day. I don't think he'll ever be the same.

Did I cause the pain by exposing him to the real world? No, but I let it impact him. I let him hurt for the purpose of godly growth.

Problem Solving

Kids in single-parent homes lack one role model. What's missing is the opportunity to watch two "mature" adults engage in conflict, solve problems, and work through crises. I would venture to say that in many, if not most, homes the two adults work through their problems in a way that tears each other down. Like our own kids, as children, most of us never learned healthy problem-solving techniques.

So, if we want to look at the bright side, maybe our kids are spared having to observe their parents rip at each other or living in a home filled with silent tension.

Then how do our kids learn problem-solving techniques? What did Paul mean when he wrote, ". . .work out your salvation" (Philippians 2:12)?

Our kids learn how to solve problems by example and by doing it themselves. They don't learn when we're always jumping into the middle of things.

"I haven't seen Tricia around here lately," I mentioned to Merilee one day. Not that I missed her; she was kind of a brat.

"Her mom won't let her play with me," Merilee told me. "We got in a fight a couple of weeks ago."

This didn't surprise me. In my opinion, Tricia's mother's way of working out her own frustration over our daughters' inability to carry on a conflict-free relationship caused her to jump in regularly and forbid her daughter to have contact with mine. In her mind, this solved the problem. Since they lived across the street, it could get very awkward. And what did it teach our kids? If you can't get along with someone, get rid of that person.

When we first moved in, Tricia's mother would often charge over to our house the minute I pulled into the driveway from work, to relay all of the horrible things my kids had done that particular day:

- "Grant threw a dirt clod at our garage!"
- "Travis chased our cat!"
- "Merilee deliberately rammed her bike into Darla's playhouse!"

Tricia's mother jumped into all of her kids' problems, no matter how minor. Sadly, the majority of the time, she isolated her kids from their friends. Not only were they deprived of learning how to resolve conflict but they were lonely as well.

And we all know a lot of lonely adults who, never having learned the art of problem solving in relationships, isolate themselves from those they once loved.

This will not happen in our family, if I have anything to say about it. When unhappiness surfaces in an individual member, that person must take responsibility for the unhappiness and, because it affects other relationships in the family, must decide how to resolve it.

The teen suicide statistics in our country bear out the fact that either we have not taught our children how to solve problems or they have chosen not to learn—or both. In our effort to protect our kids, we have actually sheltered them so that when a serious problem does arise, they only see one way out, and that's to bail out. Inexperienced in problem solving, the depressed child or teenager doesn't realize that many, if not most, major problems have a way of working themselves out in time. Our emotions tell us the truth about the pain, but they often lie to us about the facts in a crisis.

What exactly is problem solving? It is:

- Taking a look at all the options
- Asking yourself, "What is the loving thing to do for all involved?"
- Asking yourself, "What do I *want* to do?" (*Note:* what one wants to do may not be the loving thing to do, which is where repentance may enter in.)
- Embracing the feelings connected to the problem and riding them through, like a body surfer rides a wave (this often takes tremendous courage)
- Refusing to blame others for personal pain but taking responsibility for the feelings while holding others responsible for unloving behavior

Sound like a lot to teach our kids? A lot for them to grasp? It is. Many adults don't understand the problem-solving process. I certainly don't do it well all the time, but I do understand the process and teach it to my kids at every opportunity. Whether or not we apply it is entirely up to us as individuals.

My kids once had a baby-sitter I'll call Edna. When we get into our reminiscing mode, invariably someone brings up Edna and her problem-solving procedures. "Now, children, it's time to solve a prooooob-lem," Dwight will say in a whiney voice.

"Problem-solving time," Merilee will add.

"Remember that one problem we solved for three hours?" from Travis. Apparently, Edna (an older lady) would line all five of my kids up along the fireplace hearth and make them solve problems by the hour. These stories are always quite amusing, but I know I'm not receiving a compliment when one of my kids compares me with Edna, which happens too often.

Edna might have carried it to an extreme. Still, that doesn't negate the fact that, if at all possible, we must stay current with one another, bringing resolution to unhappiness in the midst of problems, if we can.

This always starts with taking personal responsibility.

Personal Responsibility

Before my kids could even reason, I was teaching them about taking responsibility for themselves and letting others do the same. I remember a time when Merilee was about five and Grant was about seven. They were building a block tower.

"Grandma doesn't like my new haircut," Merilee told Grant in a depressed tone.

"Well, whose problem is that?" was Grant's immediate response.

"Grandma's," she answered quickly.

And they went on to another subject. I smiled. I knew something was getting through.

I have to admit that taking responsibility for my personal problems in life is an ongoing challenge. It's so much easier to blame someone or something outside of myself. And it's true that others do contribute to our pain and discomfort. I never want to underestimate my kids' pain, no matter what the source.

Yet, in order to gut through the pain, in order to discover what God has for us during it and on the other side,
we must acknowledge that it's *our* pain, that we are the
ones who choose how to direct it. Blaming others gets us
nowhere because we have no control over what they've
done or may continue to do to hurt us.

I have only brief moments to ponder these kinds of
truths because, as you know, single parents are tossed
from crisis to crisis, as a ship is tossed from wave to wave
in a raging storm. The storm itself is a major crisis, as
single parenting is a constant crisis of sorts. It never really
lets up.

"Mom, Mom!" Merilee rushed in the house after school
one day, sobbing. "Mom, these boys just called me flat
chested. They were laughing—you wouldn't believe the
stuff they said."

"That's ridiculous," I said angrily. "You're only ten
years old, for Pete's sake. What do they expect—Dolly
Parton?"

That was kind of funny. We both laughed, in spite of
the seriousness of the situation.

"You know, you could have just told them that—that
you are only ten—and—"

"Oh, Mother! Right!" Merilee cried, mortified at what I
thought would have been a creative response. "I hate
them. They're always standing there after school when I
walk home. They're geeks—"

This discussion was headed in a nonproductive
direction.

"What are you going to do about them?" I asked. "I
suppose you ran away crying today."

"Well, I didn't let them see me—"

"What are you going to do tomorrow when they laugh and point at your flat chest?"

"I don't have a flat chest!" she screamed at me.

That was a debatable point, but I decided not to pursue it. Besides, creativity was hitting again.

"You know, next time they do it, you could just start laughing and pointing at *their* flat chests."

"Oh, Mom, give it up," Merilee moaned.

"Well, what are you going to do? I mean, this is your—"

"I know, I know," she interrupted. "This is my problem."

She'd been hearing that all her life, after all. Yes, those boys were being mean. But their meanness was their problem. Her grief over their meanness was her problem.

I can't honestly remember how this situation resolved itself, whether they continued to torment her or not. All I do remember is the fun and laughter we shared as we tried to come up with a creative solution to *Merilee's* problem.

Unfortunately, refusing to blame others for our problems, resisting self-protective behavior in the midst of our problems, and taking responsibility for our feelings about others connected to our problems present an ongoing challenge. No, happiness is not the goal. Love is.

So we "happily" achieve the goal of loving our kids by resisting the ever-present urge to "take care" of them in their problems. But then one of our precious offspring spurns that love and rejects us—deliberately, without flinching—and we plunge into a chasm of our own painful unhappiness. We swallow our own lectures. How do we gut through the pain of a child's abandonment?

7
YOU CAN'T MEAN THAT

When It Feels Like Rejection

"Mom, I keep waiting for you to turn into some kind of a monster." Twelve-year-old Travis stared at me intently, yet lovingly, as we sat together on his bed one evening.

"What? What do you mean?"

"Well, my friends all hate their parents. You should hear how they talk about them. I keep thinking that one of these days you're going to turn into the kind of mom my friends talk about and I'll hate you." He looked puzzled. "It's not happening."

I chuckled. "Travis, I've been waiting for the same thing . . . a monster to emerge. All my friends just tolerate their kids your age. They fight constantly and are basically just waiting for them to grow up and leave home. Isn't that sad?"

"So we're both waiting to hate the other one?" Travis laughed. "That's funny. What if it never happens?"

I put my arm around my son. "It doesn't ever have to happen. We've built something solid."

Yet, exactly one year later, as I watched Travis and all of his belongings pile into his father's car and drive away from me, I wished I could hate him. It would make losing him so much easier. (*See* chapter ten for the complete story.)

Was my son rejecting me in favor of his father? Did he unconsciously hate me? How could he so easily leave me if he loved me? Was his leaving a real or a perceived rejection? Suddenly the answers to these questions were vitally important. Were there answers? Would the answers reveal my glaring weaknesses and failure as a mother?

Rejection and abandonment feelings may be the most intense feelings we ever experience. So intense are they that few of us really enter into them. Whether child or adult, we often look for an escape the minute the feeling begins to surface.

When we're rejected, whether we're closely related to the rejector or not, the first and utmost important question that surfaces is, "Does that person's reason for rejecting me mean (gulp) that there is something inherently *wrong* with me?"

I do believe a strange and wonderful bond exists between a mother and her child. When either one rejects the other, even momentarily, something shatters deep inside both of them and is never quite the same.

For a single mom, her child's rejection penetrates deeper than the sharpest sword, because she has already suffered so much rejection and abandonment in her relationship with the child's father.

I firmly believe this is why so many parents and children are estranged from each other from the child's teen years into adulthood. At the first sign of rejection of one by the other, both begin to build walls to protect themselves. For survival's sake, each must blame the other or stand emotionally naked in front of the other, with no walls, and face the fearsome possibility that something may be *wrong* with the self. Someone might have to take responsibility for the inflicting of pain. Someone might have to repent. Someone might have to forgive. Someone might have to (horrors!) change. No one can face that, so—

The walls grow higher. But everyone wears a nice smile at family gatherings. They may remember birthdays and celebrate holidays. They discuss newspaper items, world affairs, and career choices, while down deep, unresolved rejection feelings fester—and hate, for either oneself or other family members, grows.

It's a painful scenario, one that we single parents with young children can prevent if we can own our rejection feelings (real or imagined), acknowledge and confront them, and let them go, choosing to forgive and love in the face of rejection. It's a tough assignment. We may not want to do this, until we look at the alternatives, which are more loneliness and isolation than we have ever known.

Imagined or Real

Is the pain we suffer from rejection any less intense because the rejection is imagined? When a beloved child shouts, "I hate you!" is that what is really meant? Whether it is or isn't, how easy is it to simply say, "Oh, dear, I know you don't mean that," smile, and walk away?

I don't know about you, but I have a hard time separating my kids' momentary emotionally cruel outbursts from what might be deep-seated unresolved bitterness or hatred. Whatever the cause, the feeling I receive from the rejecting interaction is real, and it hurts. There is no denying the pain.

Determining whether the rejection is real or not is important in deciding how to deal with it. Sometimes with imagined rejection, it's simply a matter of getting a perspective. But it's not that simple with real rejection. Real rejection requires much more internal processing of feelings, interaction with the rejector (if possible), telling ourselves the truth, forgiving, making choices to love anyway, and so forth.

Imagined rejection is when your kid:

- Forgets your birthday but remembers Bart Simpson's
- Refuses to eat, wear, or do something at your suggestion but will eat, wear, or do the same thing at Johnny's or Susie's suggestion
- Perceives you as a mental-institution escapee and treats you as such
- Never says more to you than "Hello, what's for dinner?" but talks for hours on the phone with friends

These rejections can be explained in the order in which they appear above: Your kid is either distracted, exerting his or her independence, mentally unbalanced and projecting on you, or disinterested in anything that doesn't concern himself or herself personally. The child isn't really rejecting you as much as simply growing up. It's unrealistic for us to expect this process to be neat and tidy. In order to grow up, the child must go through the process of rejecting many of the parents' values, ways of thinking and doing things, ways of being and living. As parents, we don't have to interpret this as the child rejecting us, although that's what it may feel like.

Real rejection is when your kid:

- Decides you're the enemy and sets up an adversarial relationship
- Becomes angry at you and lets his or her anger turn to bitterness
- Writes you off as stupid, ugly, and/or old and refuses to relate to you in any way
- Turns his or her back on you in order to join his or her dad's side (ouch!)

We can take control of imagined rejection; with real rejection, we have very little control. In our family, we have suffered both kinds. What's imagined hurts no less than what's real. The first thing we must do to get through either imagined or real rejection is to embrace the pain.

Embrace the Pain

"Embrace the pain? Are you kidding? Pain hurts." This was my response when a friend once advised me to ride the waves of grief. Why would I want to embrace something that hurts me?

I soon found out why by experiencing the effects of denied suffering on my personal guts and relationships with others. When we allow ourselves to feel our pain, then express it, we can be healed. If not, our pain poisons our relationships at their very roots.

One by one, all three of my boys have left to go live with their father. Each time I passed an empty bedroom, it screamed rejection at me. The voices within cried out every time I crept by:

- "He left you."
- "He loves his dad more."
- "You've lost him. He's gone for good."
- "You just *thought* you had a relationship. Look how easily he tossed you aside."
- "You had your chance. You blew it. You didn't love him enough to make him stay."
- "And he didn't love you."
- "What's wrong with you, anyway, that you can't even keep your kids?"

The truth is, there was nothing *wrong* with me. My boys were simply making choices based on their personal needs, which had nothing to do with my value in their lives.

But it's difficult to see the truth when rejection feelings are piercing your heart.

If rejection feelings dominated our relationships with our own parents when we were children, we will relate to our children out of those unhealed feelings.

Just recently, as my own mother lay in a hospital bed dying of cancer, I finally embraced the pain of rejection I'd felt in my relationship with her all my life. I let her see my pain. To my surprise, deep down, underneath the pain, I found love—the most intense, passionate, warm kind of love I could imagine.

"Mom, I really love you," I sobbed for the first time in my thirty-nine years, with my heart engaged.

"I love you, too," she answered without hesitation. And then, for the first time ever, she let me see and feel her own pain of rejection. "You know, every morning I would wake up and think, *I don't have a daughter anymore.*"

I stared at her in disbelief. She cared; she really *cared*

whether or not she had a daughter. This was news. This was good news. This was the most wonderful news in the world. My mother cared about me.

I knew my relationships with my little girls and my growing boys would never be the same, and they haven't been.

Suddenly, I believe it's absolutely crucial in the unit that we let one another see and feel the pain that we cause by our hurting words and actions. We must realize that rejection of one another hurts. I hope to head off the years of potential break in relationship with any one of my kids because of repressed rejection feelings in either myself or them.

In order to do that, each of us must embrace our own feelings of rejection and, more often than we feel comfortable or safe with, express our feelings to one another. As we sift through the rejection, we have hope of uncovering the love that has been there all along.

Every once in a while it works. But unless we risk embracing and expressing the pain, we'll never know.

Merilee, Amber, and Travis had a rough day recently. Travis and Amber had ganged up on Merilee unmercifully; Merilee reacted like a cornered animal. It all culminated at the end of the day with Amber grabbing her blanket and pillow out of the room she shared with Merilee and going to sleep in Travis's room.

Merilee was not happy with this arrangement. "You can't do that!" Merilee screamed, outraged. "I hate sleeping alone. I'm sleeping in there with you guys."

"No way!" Travis returned. "Not after the way you [acted, treated us, lied, or whatever]." Fill in the blank; they repeat this basic dialogue regularly.

Well, Merilee did her freak-out routine, to Travis and

Amber's satisfaction. She ranted. She raved. She slammed doors. All while her brother and sister, totally unconcerned, watched a little TV before they went to sleep.

I knew Merilee hated sleeping alone. She was afraid of monsters in the night. She also felt horribly rejected by Travis and Amber. Was the rejection imagined or real? They were the only ones who knew for sure. Either way, she hurt.

When the situation had calmed down some and Merilee's anger was fully spent, I suggested she embrace her pain. I prodded and poked where angels (and demons) fear to tread.

"What are you afraid of? Do you feel rejected? I bet this hurts. Do you feel alone?" And then the unthinkable: "Maybe you could tell them about your fear and ask them if—"

"Aaaaargh! Are you kidding?! They don't care about my. . . ."

That was the crucial issue. Did they or did they not care? I knew I was asking her to take a risk I probably wouldn't even take myself, considering all that had happened that day.

I eased off but returned a few moments later with the same suggestion. "It's a risk, I know," I finished, backing out of her room. Then I shrugged. "But what do you have to lose? At this point, you'll be sleeping alone anyway." I left the room.

A few moments later, I heard her knock on Travis's door, then, "The reason I want to sleep with you guys is because I'm afraid to sleep alone in my room. Could I?"

"Sure," Travis said. "Just move that stuff over against the wall."

Even I was amazed. Nothing ever went so smoothly.

"It worked." She beamed at me as she ran into her room to get her sleeping bag.

Every once in a while things in our family work out the way they're supposed to. It always surprises me.

Letting Go

Maybe single parents need their kids to love them even more than "nuclear" parents. I'm sure we put way too much pressure on our kids to meet our needs because of the absence of intimacy with a mate. (Not that the presence of a mate would mean automatic intimacy. I entertain no fantasies there.)

But we just may tend to clutch, grasp, and cling a little more than a family where the parents have each other as well as the kids. Because of this, rejection hits us a bit harder. As we have learned to embrace the pain, so we must learn to let go of it so we are not devastated by it, just as we let go of our kids while they let go of us.

That should be fairly simple, shouldn't it? Once embracing our pain, why would we choose to hang onto it, anyway? There are a number of reasons:

- As long as we cling to the pain, we cling to the one causing it. We still hold the person in our grasp.
- We continue to control the situation, in a sick kind of way.
- The possibility of gaining the other party's sympathy stays alive.
- We may be able to make the other person feel guilty enough for causing us pain, thereby giving us our way in the situation.
- Nursing our pain gives us sweet revenge.

These are very normal responses. But if we are at all committed to doing our part to establish healthy and functional families, we must commit ourselves to the healing that will naturally follow the pain if we can let go.

The pain of rejection clicks in after one of any number of words and/or feelings our little imps so casually toss out:

- "You burnt the toast."
- "I'm moving out."
- "I can do that myself, thanks."
- "Bug off."
- Silences. Long silences.
- Looks. Hateful looks.
- Withdrawals. Painful withdrawals.

After we decide whether it's imagined rejection on our part or real rejection and embrace the pain of it, letting it hurt, we can let go of it. Which means offering forgiveness, grace, understanding, and compassion for the woundedness in the child that caused the rejection in the first place.

I can't stress enough the importance of letting go of the pain from deep down. It is the *only* way to uncover the love that will carry us through the painful times in relationship with our kids.

In a movie I watched recently about a mother-daughter relationship, I could see clearly the close connection between love and hate. These two simultaneously loved and hated each other many times a day. It doesn't have to be that way between kids and their parents, but too often it is. I think we too often deny hateful feelings because allowing them seems so sinful. The problem is that whether we allow them or not, they still surface from time to time. We are doing ourselves and our kids a terrible disservice to pretend this never happens. Our hearts can't heal unless we acknowledge and deal with our *true* feelings, no matter how uncomfortable they are or how sinful they seem.

Along with offering forgiveness, grace, understanding, and compassion in the face of rejection, above and beyond that, letting go means to choose to love, to move in love toward the source of pain, toward the rejecting child. Ouch.

Choosing to Love

Everything we've discussed in this book so far and will discuss in future chapters ends up at the same place: choosing to love. Unless all members of the family can ultimately make this choice, the family will stagnate: Movement will cease, self-protection will set in, defenses will go up; anger will turn to bitterness and bitterness will erode the foundation of relationships in the family.

Choosing to love sounds so simple. If asked, I hardly know of a parent who wouldn't confess, "Of course, I love my kids." But do we really? And what does it mean to love in the face of rejection? I see so many parents working hard to please their kids so as not to experience the rejection that is sure to follow if they are ever the cause of their kids' unhappiness. Is that love? I see desperate, panicky parents, single parents who pour their whole selves into their kids, so terrified are they of doing something wrong and getting rejected for it.

It was Carl Jung who said, "Neurosis is always a substitute for legitimate suffering." If we refuse to legitimately suffer, the best we can hope for is a neurotic relationship with our kids, one based on fear of loss. Not a pretty picture. We are left at the mercy of our children.

But the power of God's love can never be underestimated. It breaks down impenetrable barriers.

I wonder if cynicism is possible for kids. I wonder if kids in single-parent units can become cynical about love so young. After all, kids from divorced homes like ours are daily faced with the reality that the once-young couple (their parents) who promised to love each other forever didn't—they broke their promise. Someone, maybe both someones, let love die. How are the kids left to interpret that? Big deal if you choose to love today; you can always change your mind tomorrow. Or the one you chose to love dies and you wish you hadn't loved, it hurts so bad to lose. Can our kids really believe us when we say "I love you" in the face of rejection? Do we have the right to say that when love wasn't strong enough to hold two grown people together?

I know of no kind of love stronger than love offered in the face of rejection. It's not perfect love; it's tough, committed love, the kind that's steady, constant, unshakable. It's choosing to hurt, because the receiver is not listening or caring or sometimes not even present to know one way or the other. At the risk of sounding too melodramatic, it's the kind of love Jesus offered to all those who crucified Him and all those who would crucify Him anew in the future. Only God can initiate this kind of love.

Sometimes I hate being an adult all the time. Kids always have an excuse: they don't understand, they're immature, they have yet to learn whatever it is.

But as the adult, as the parent, I'm the one who must always choose to love, no matter what my kids do:

- They erect huge walls in a minute. I have to refuse to put up even a brick.

- They blurt out their angry feelings. I must direct mine "appropriately."
- They can run away from home if they choose to (but they'd better not, if they know what's good for them). I must hang in there no matter what.

I can't wait until my kids have kids and they begin to feel even a little of what it's like to have to be the responsible person all the time—the one with no excuses, no escapes, no exit doors. The one who must or (better worded) gets to love . . . and love . . . and love again.

What a wonderful privilege, really. What an honor. I haven't always had this choice. I used to be a kid. When rejected, my only choice was to close off and reject back.

Without the choice to love, our family would be one huge gaping wound.

My kids are catching on. I watch my mature teenage son regularly initiate love with his younger sister when she is unable to receive it and openly rejects him. I'm so proud of him.

Although feelings of rejection are a very real part of the single-parenting process, that's not all there is. We must keep a perspective and remember that this thing can be a lot of fun. That, too, is our choice.

8
WE'RE OUTA' HERE

When to Hang On Is to Cut Loose

Oscar Wilde once said, "Life is too important to be taken seriously."

How true that is. It's just that single parenting can be so heavy, so serious, so alone. Well, that's one perspective. Another perspective is that single parenting is too important to be taken seriously.

As children, the seriousness of life penetrated our souls. From adults, we heard:

- "Wipe that smirk off your face," in an angry tone
- "What's so funny?" in an angry tone
- "This is very serious," in a somber tone

Or we watched adults live seriously. So as we grew up, we decided that getting married and having a family was serious.

The kid kinds of demands and responsibilities on me as a single mother take their daily toll. How do I disentangle myself from the daily teaching, chauffeuring, counseling, cooking, disciplining, cleaning, and refereeing for just a moment to get a perspective on this thing?

Getting a Perspective

What does it mean to get a perspective? To me, it means to distance myself from the situation so I can see the amusing reality, the not-so-heavy-or-serious reality.

In the Shakespearean sense, I figure I get only two choices, two ways of looking at life: as a tragedy or a comedy. Which would you prefer? (I did ask a melancholic friend this question recently and she said, "a tragedy.")

To get a perspective is to:

- Laugh at life
- Lighten up in one's approach
- Relax
- Accept the deep chasm of both pain and joy

The reality is that whenever you have more than one person under one roof at a time, you face the potential for heaviness and perpetual conflict. We have many more than one person under our roof. With all of these people bumping into one another at regular intervals, is getting a perspective even possible?

"It's true! I did it! I deserve the electric chair!" This confession came from my sobbing son moments after the police hauled him home for lobbing a rock through a car window to the tune of $333.00, two court appearances, and eight hours of community service.

"Mom, it hurts!" This came from another sobbing son who hobbled into the house one snowy morning from his paper route after being hit by a car.

"Mom, I can't find her anywhere!" This came from my sobbing daughter on the phone (I was on a trip), who couldn't locate her younger sister late one night.

And I'm supposed to get and keep a perspective?

I'm discovering that a perspective can be an illusive commodity. It's something we find, then lose, then find again, then lose.

It's important that we become aware of when we're losing our perspective so we can take strides to find it again. You know you're losing it when your kid:

- Stubs her toe and you rush her to the emergency room
- Burps at the dinner table and you ground him for a week
- Shoves someone in the school lunch line and you take her to therapy for the next six months

When we lose our perspective we often strike a fatal blow to the unit's ability to have fun together.

What causes us to lose our perspective? Many culprits surface here and there, thrusting us into the "heaviness" of single parenting. I see four major thieves of the unit's fun.

Crisis and the Resulting Panic

We must make room for the element of surprise in our single-parenting role. Around every corner of every day I encounter a surprise—an unexpected happening, event, person. If I can keep myself from panicking, I can keep my perspective.

"Mom, my teacher says I have lice. Would you check?"

"Mom, I have to turn in ninety-five dollars by the end of next week for our three-day field trip." (Ninety-five dollars? I'm trying to scrounge up lunch money for tomorrow.)

"Mom, you know that glass candle holder in the dining room? The one you loved so much?" (What's this? *Loved?* Past tense?)

Hold on. Don't panic. It's only lice, only ninety-five dollars, only a glass candle holder. Keep a perspective. God is still alive, still rotating the world, still loving us—madly.

Yes, these difficulties do affect our momentary perceptions of life. And these are reasonably light ones, compared to things like drug abuse, teen pregnancies, and deadly diseases, which do occur from time to time.

God still loves us madly. Don't panic. Stay cool.

In Jesus' words, "Do not let your hearts be troubled. Trust in God" (John 14:1).

Try to see each crisis as an opportunity to grow in trust. Your kids are watching you.

Burnout

Our perspective slips away as the daily grind weakens our ability to endure. What to do?

Stop. Rest.

Rest? With five kids? Yeah, right.

To burn out is to rush home from work to run your kids back and forth to soccer, jobs, and Campfire Girls, cook dinner, help with homework, lead the unit in some kind of spiritual time, settle endless disputes, chase the dog, who accidentally got loose, ad nauseam—all alone. Suddenly one day you can't get out of bed, and you don't even care.

How do we recapture our perspective when we don't care if we ever get out of bed?

- Disneyland (seriously, I go there twice a year—it's amazing how quickly the tired child in me comes to life)
- Christmas—if you have money for presents and energy to go get them
- Winning the lottery

If none of the above is possible, we're back to trusting God (John 14:1). Which is actually a good place to start, but one that many of us don't consider until a crisis hits.

Stop and rest. The world (and your kids) will still be there when you start moving again.

Reality

Nothing like a strong dose of reality to cause us to lose our perspective. Reality? What kind of reality?

I'm a single parent with five kids. I don't know about you, but that's enough to do me in. If I dwell on that too long and too deeply, I begin to labor under the responsibility (sometimes I hate that word) and my perspective starts to slide. I begin to teach, train, and discipline instead of love and have fun. My kids feel it, too, and their interactions with one another become more tense.

What to do?

Trust God? Absolutely. Trust Him with our reality. He's quite familiar with it, as He lives here with us.

"But God," you might wonder, "what if I miss an opportunity to teach, train, or discipline Johnny or Susie?"

So? Do it next time. Just don't miss the opportunity to love, to hug, to have fun, to live in passion-filled reality with your kids.

In order to do so, keep your perspective.

Our Kids

This particular cause for losing our perspective could actually fall under any of the previous categories: crisis, burnout, or reality. I give our kids a separate heading here because they have the unique ability to cause us to lose our perspective by losing theirs. We have to watch for that.

We all know that with kids, a hangnail or a scraped knee is a big deal, not to mention the loss of a friend or a move to a different desk in the classroom.

It's tough, because kids engage their emotions every time a crisis hits, just as do most of us women. If one of our kids has a crisis during our PMS week, we're sunk.

This may not be accurate, but I tend to feel that men are much better at keeping a perspective than women. They look at situations so logically and rationally. Our unit has definitely been at a disadvantage in this area at times.

What a blessing to have my seventeen-year-old son living with us again. I regain my perspective every time he says, "Mom, it's not that big a deal." Or "Mom, look at it this way. . . ." Or especially, "Mom, keep it in perspective."

Which brings us back to trusting God. From His perspective, situations look very different indeed. A scraped knee simply gives Him an opportunity to express His love by healing, as does a broken heart. He's an expert at those. A frown? I can just see Him clasping His hands in glee at the opportunity to arrange circumstances for the specific purpose of bringing a smile.

Yes, keeping a perspective is crucial if we consider life and single parenting too important to take seriously. The knowledge that God has a time and season for everything under the sun should give us a sense of security when we worry about whether or not we're taking it all seriously enough.

Time to Weep, Time to Laugh

I scurried around the office, completing last-minute work assignments so I could get out of there on time. A friend and I planned to take another friend out to dinner that evening for her birthday, and there was no time to waste.

Just as I headed out the door, the phone rang.

"Mom?" It was Travis. "The cops are on their way here. Amber and Eric decided to play post office today, you know?"

"Yes. . . ." My heart waited in the dark. What was coming?

"They stole all the mail out of the neighbors' mailboxes, took it down to their fort, opened it, wrote on it, tore it up, threw it around—"

"Okay, okay," I stopped him. "I'm on my way home."

Intense feelings crashed in on me as I sped the four miles home:

- Fury. How could Amber do such a thing? Certainly she knew it was wrong.
- Blame. Why wasn't Travis watching her more closely? I'd left him in charge.
- Humiliation. How could I ever face the neighbors again?
- Guilt. I'd failed as a mother. A good parent's child would never do something so horrible.

How would I handle this? A husband/father would know what to do. At times like this I wished I had one of those creatures.

The cops. Wasn't tampering with the mail a federal offense? Would they take Amber to jail? How silly. No,
they'd take *me* to jail; they'd take Amber to a juvenile
home. Our family would be split apart. How awful. It was
truly amazing how your life could change so drastically in
a few moments.

I pulled into our street, expecting to see a couple of
police cars, lights flashing, and a mob of hostile neighbors
on the front lawn, waiting to lynch me and my daughter,
the felon.

But it was fairly quiet as I drove into the driveway. No
police cars. No neighbors. Just the usual kid noises from
inside the house.

"Where is she?" I cried crazily to Travis, who sat on the
couch watching cartoons. "What's happening? Did the
cops take her away already?"

"Huh?" Travis looked at me blankly. "Oh, you mean
Amber? The mail thief? She's in her room, awaiting the
sentencing."

"Where are the cops?"

"They left when they found out the mail thief was only
five years old."

I didn't know whether to laugh or cry. Was this a time
for sorrow or joy?

Amber appeared in the doorway. "What's my punishment?"

My daughter, tear-lined face, grubby jeans, and all, was
still a part of our family. We were still all together. Relief
washed over me as all my irrational thoughts about jail
and the breakup of our unit dissipated. What I was left
with was the harsh reality of dealing with the small mail
thief standing before me and the neighbors.

It was time to weep.

Amber's punishment was to face the neighbors and take responsibility for her crime. We trudged from house to house, and I made her repeat three phrases to whomever answered the door.

"I'm sorry I stole your mail."

"I'll never do it again."

"Will you forgive me?"

The neighbors were much more gracious than we deserved. They had recovered some of their mail and obviously saw no productive reason to vent their frustration at the small person who stood, repentant, on their porch.

I did take my friend out for her birthday dinner, and as I relayed the afternoon's traumatic events, I knew it was time to laugh.

"There is a time for everything, and a season for every activity under heaven . . . a time to weep and a time to laugh" (Ecclesiastes 3:1, 4).

Sometimes it's hard to know when to do what. It gets confusing. Kids can say and do such funny things, yet those funny things can often have serious ramifications. What if I do the "wrong" thing at the "wrong" time? Burst out in guffaws at a serious moment or shake my head sadly when the situation is more worthy of a chuckle?

Again, there is no right or wrong response here, only loving or unloving ones, honest or dishonest ones, real or phony ones.

I cried daily tears of despair and anguish the first few years of my venture into single parenting. I found nothing funny, nothing to laugh about in those days. Sometimes I wondered if I'd ever laugh again. So did my kids.

It was a long, long season of weeping. Too long.

My kids lived with a shell of what had once been their fun-loving mother.

"Mom, are you still in there?" I could hear my kids' plaintive cry off in the distance somewhere, across the tear-filled moat of my hopelessness.

Yet, slowly, steadily, surely, God concentrated on letting down the drawbridge where my kids and I would one day meet in the middle.

He did and we did. We're laughing now—a lot. It's the time, the season for laughing.

That doesn't mean we have ceased weeping. Not at all. We have wonderful moments of both laughter and weeping, but my tears no longer separate us, and our tears are never without hope.

I get criticized sometimes for not taking this single-parenting thing seriously enough, but what my critics don't understand is that this unit has graduated from the School of Grief. We have earned the privilege of laughing long and loud.

Cultivating the Unit's Sense of Humor

Everyone has a sense of humor, but some of us need permission to express it, and many of us need someone else to bring it out. Having experienced the need for isolation recently, I have learned to amuse myself when no one else is around. But this does not come naturally, especially for children, who are constantly being told by adults how they "should" be acting or feeling.

Just this week at a parent-teacher conference, Merilee's teacher, with a twinkle in his eye, told me, "You know, Merilee is not at all afraid of her feelings."

As if that were news to me. Yet, I was proud of my

daughter. She entered her feelings bravely. Oh, she had plenty to learn about "appropriate expression" (*see* chapter ten), but she was on the right track.

It's true that we must teach our children about "the time to weep and the time to laugh." I find that it's such a delicate balance—freeing our children to express themselves while simultaneously teaching them to watch out for others. Even as an adult, I know that my unreined, raw passion can make others uncomfortable. But I so desperately desire my kids to be free to be who God created; I would rather they err on the side of freedom than lose their true selves while striving to please everyone around them.

In order to cultivate the unit's sense of humor, our kids must feel free to express themselves without fear of ridicule. It's tricky, because if there's one thing kids seem to love to do, it's ridicule one another.

Unless they're gross, I *always* laugh at my kids' jokes. Everyone else in the unit will usually either groan or say something mean; someone has to affirm the joker's effort to be funny.

Jokes are surface efforts. What needs to happen deep down so the members of the unit can laugh together?

- Each of us must first be able to laugh at himself or herself. If we can't laugh at ourselves, we have no business poking fun at others (and others are often the brunt of our humor).
- We must realize that we can *choose* to love or hate, to laugh or cry, to live or die. We can choose to feel sorry for ourselves or to have fun.
- We must unconditionally accept both ourselves and the other members of the unit. Laughter will not

ring out free and merry unless we do. Where judgment and ridicule are allowed, the laughter is caus-
tic and hollow, but where acceptance reigns, the
laughter is bonding.

• We must tune in to the unit's corporate sense of
  humor or be left behind. I am still trying to teach
  Merilee, with little success, not to take things so
  seriously, that we all love to tease, and that those
  who put up the worst fuss get teased the most. She
  hasn't quite learned this rhythm. She still gets
  teased the most.

Our areas of insecurity keep us supersensitive. I have
absolutely no artistic ability in my hands, but what can I
do when my children come to me year after year, pleading
for help on an art project or costume? Compassion wins
out, and I help. And they always wish I hadn't. Do I laugh
or cry when my kids' brainchild always gets the booby
prize? I've stopped crying. It's more fun to laugh.

It's fairly easy to cultivate the unit's sense of humor.
Because you're a single-parent family, you alone set the
rhythm and pace. You need wait for no one's approval.
Simply start laughing about everything and nothing. Find
the funny side of the most serious situation, and when it's
time, share the humor with your kids. Most likely, they've
already tuned in.

Playing Together

Grant burst into the room, interrupting my profound
musings and the letter I was writing to a friend. "Mom, I
gotta go frog hunting tonight. Will you take me?"

"What? Frog hunting? What do you mean you gotta go
frog hunting?"

"I found this great swamp. I just know it's full of frogs. But they only come out at night. We have to go after dark."

"Absolutely not." I turned back to the letter I was writing. "You know you can't go out after dark."

Grant sighed. "I know. That's why I'm asking you to take me."

"Take you?" I guess I hadn't heard that part. "Take you frog hunting? After dark? Yeah, right." I smiled and patted his shoulder. *Isn't that what dads are supposed to do?* I thought but didn't say. "I have plans tonight, honey." Plans to relax, put up my feet, read a good book. . . .

"You can't take me?" He looked crestfallen, absolutely devastated. "All those good frogs. . . ."

Wasted. All those good frogs, just wasted. All those croaking, wonderful, hopping, fun frogs. I imagined what he must be thinking.

All those slimy, ugly, swampy, smelly frogs. I moved into my own thoughts now. Ugh. . . .

"Mom, please," he pleaded. "It won't take us long. I know right where they are."

My imaginings now took me to a swampy frog nest (or whatever you call a frog's home), where I saw humongous frogs leaping out at me, their slimy hides bouncing off me. I shivered.

I wished Grant's dad didn't live so far away. Was there anyone else? A neighbor? A friend? A frog lover nearby? Desperate, I wracked my brain for the answer.

But deep down I already knew the answer. I tried to run, but like a frog, the answer leapt out at me everywhere. It was too late to run. It was time to put away the adult in me. It was time to free the child in me. It was time to play with my son.

"How about a game of Parcheesi tonight?" I tried. One last-ditch attempt.

Grant shook his head.

It wasn't what I had planned for that evening, but I'm a single mom. Single moms don't always get to do what they have planned. I thought dark would never come. It must have been the longest day of the year—June something.

Ten o'clock was pitch black. I crept behind my friend, Barb, whom I had roped into coming with us and who held our only flashlight. Grant led us along the edge of the swamp, searching the murky waters for the "best" frogs. Squish, squish went our shoes through the mud. Croak, croak, went the frogs as they protested the invasion of their turf. Pound, pound, went my heart as I waited to be attacked by killer frogs.

"There's one!" Grant yelled. Barb swung the flashlight around and flooded the area to which he'd pointed with light. Grant quickly bent down, scooped up the inch-long creature (and that was one of the "best" ones), and dropped him (her?) into the orange plastic Halloween pumpkin Barb carried.

"Aaaaargh!" Barb and I screamed at the risk of the frog leaping into our faces before she could cover the top of the pumpkin with tinfoil.

We repeated this process many times over. By about the sixth or seventh time, Barb and I were no longer screaming in terror but were as excited as Grant at every capture.

We were playing.

No, it wasn't what I had planned; play usually isn't. We don't often plan to play. Maybe we should. Most often play happens when we're engaged in other activities. It happens when we:

- Follow a child's meanderings (physical or mental)
- Risk putting away the responsible adult inside us to free the spontaneous child
- Forget about our to-do list
- Live in the present
- Quit worrying about age, appearance, dignity

It happens when we really know that "life is too important to take seriously," that play is for adults, that this moment is all we have for sure.

Whether it's hunting for frogs in summer, rolling in leaves in fall, building a snowman in winter, or riding a bike in spring, when the moment beckons us to play, we must take heed. Such moments pass too quickly.

9
DID YOU SAY HE LOOKED AT YOU FUNNY?

Settling Endless Disputes

"Mom, Travis just called Danny a dork!" Merilee wailed from her bedroom. "Make him stop! I can't stand it!" Thump! Bang! "Get out of my bedroom!" Pause. "Mom!"

Danny? Danny who? I was sure I didn't have a kid named Danny, and I couldn't remember any of my kids' friends being named Danny. I wracked my brain as I hurried to Merilee's bedroom, where Travis stood in the doorway pointing to a poster on his sister's wall and laughing hysterically.

"Mom, he's making fun of Danny!" Merilee cried. "Do something!"

Danny . . . oh yes, a member of a current pop rock group that Merilee idolized. I looked more closely at the poster.

"Mom, he is a dork," Travis choked out between guffaws. "Look at him standing there, his chest out, his hands in his pockets, trying to look all macho—"

"Mom!"

"Travis, it's not nice to ridicule someone your sister admires." I began rather weakly for what was obviously a serious situation escalating in intensity by the moment. It was just that—well, the lanky kid on the poster did look kind of dorky, now that Travis mentioned it.

"Mom, Dwight won't let me in the bathroom, and I really have to go," I heard from another part of the house.

Pound, pound!

The phone rang then. Relieved, I hoped the phone might distract someone—anyone. Instead, "Mom, tell Grant to get off the phone so I can talk. He keeps making belching noises."

Travis was still laughing at Danny and. . . .

I slipped out of the house quietly and was never heard from again.

Not really, but at particularly stressful times, I like to fantasize. If I were to desert the ship, where would I go? Who would I be? Do I really want to be the first one in the unit to bail out? After all I've taught my kids about commitment, love, hanging in there during the rough times?

As single parents, how do we weather the storms? Without anyone else to help shoulder the load, how do we handle and resolve all the conflicts that come up in a given day?

A friend once informed me that among myself and my five kids, we had thirty individual interpersonal relationships going on in our home at any one time. Thirty! Was I the one responsible to make sure these thirty relationships developed healthily without deterioration into codependent, psychopathic, addictive, people-pleasing, antisocial, caretaking, incestuous, and schizophrenic behaviors? (That's what I get for taking this single-parenting thing so seriously. I have to read every new book on the market so that I know exactly what's happening when a child won't eat his asparagus or another child goes into a rage when he can't get to the third level on a Nintendo game.)

When I was married, I could send the kids to their father to settle at least half of a day's disputes. He may or may not have contributed a positive resolution to the situation, but having the option saved my sanity. With thirty interpersonal relationships, you can imagine how often a seemingly insignificant interaction between two or more parties quickly erupted into a volatile dispute. Correction: Counting their father, make that forty-two interpersonal relationships.

I no longer have that option: I'm it.

Looking at this realistically, there is absolutely no way I can take part in or break up every single fight in our home. If so, that is all I would do all day long. I don't know how Susanna Wesley did it with eighteen children.

What I want to know is if, just *if*, my kids were left to themselves, if I didn't interfere the minute someone yelled "Mom!" what would happen? Would a scowl on a face harden permanently? Would eyes stay crossed forever? Would one child twist another's arm until it was out of the socket? I mean, what is the worst that could happen?

Maybe they really would turn into savages and annihilate one another like in a Stephen King novel. On the other hand, maybe, just maybe, they would work the problem out all by themselves. Do I dare risk finding out?

How do I know when to jump in and when to stay out of it? As a mother, what exactly is my responsibility? How far do I let them go before I interfere? Do I use every conflict as an opportunity to train them, as the Bible instructs me to do, "making the most of every opportunity, because the days are evil"(Ephesians 5:16)?

The above questions are difficult to answer. But then maybe the answers aren't supposed to prove readily available. Maybe we are supposed to exercise the creativity God put in us and approach every dispute and relationship problem for the unique challenge it is, resting in the fact that God has promised sufficient grace for this present hour (2 Corinthians 12:9).

Sufficient grace. What a reassuring thought. God made both kids and parents; He knew we'd all need lots of grace.

Why do we hate it so much when our kids fight? What are we afraid of?

- They might do irreparable damage to one another— physical or emotional.
- People will think we aren't good parents, that we haven't trained our children well (their fighting is a reflection on our parenting).
- One or both or all of the fighters may lose control, meaning mainly that we've lost control of our kids.
- If unresolved, the fighters may come out the other side bitter and hateful.

I could name more. Underlying all of the above is the fear of failure. We fear that we have failed to teach our kids how to love. That's a valid fear, one to be taken seriously.

Until we can identify our own fear, we are ineffective as mediators, if indeed that is what the situation calls for.

We might as well face the fact that our kids will fight with one another, with their peers, with their teachers, with us. As long as we have two or more people in the home, we will have conflict. Always. The goal is not the absence of conflict.

Many of us were programmed to believe that conflict is bad, awful, horrible. Avoid conflict at all costs, people, please, hide your true feelings, forgive, sacrifice yourself, deny your real needs; do whatever it takes to ward off conflict.

It should come as good news that conflict in itself is not bad, awful, or horrible. It's how we respond to it that can be very bad, awful, or horrible. Conflict itself can prove a means of godly growth. Through it, we learn more about how to love one another.

Keeping this in mind, the goal, as I mentioned above, is not to avoid conflict but to direct it. How do we do that? How can we continue to view conflict as a positive means of growth for the unit when it appears to be ripping the family apart, limb by limb?

Cracks in the Unit

Cracks in the unit are inevitable. What we don't want to do is spiral downward into self-condemnation when this happens. That's easy to do when, for example, you attend the annual parent-teacher conference and your kid's teacher leans back in her or his chair, peers at you over her or his eyeglasses, and says in a serious tone:

"_____ [put your name in the blank], _____ [your child's name] seems to be having some trouble with the other kids in the class. I notice here on the form [one of the hundred or so that you fill out at the beginning of every school year] that you're a single parent . . ." with emphasis on the word *single*. A knowing nod. And you can imagine what follows.

It's also easy to do when you come home to find one kid choking, biting, hitting, kicking another. *Oh, it's because I'm a single parent. My poor children don't have a father. They're so deprived. There's no hope.*

Before you can spiral all the way down to the bottom, your kids are usually into some new mischievous activity.

Nevertheless, self-condemnation incapacitates you, should you feel so inclined to intervene in the scuffle. When you let yourself believe that your kids' troubles can be directly attributed to their fatherlessness, or when you let others, including your kids, convince you of that, there really is no hope outside of your getting remarried.

But the unit needs help now.

The truth is, our kids' troubles can be directly attributed to their sin nature and their unloving choices. Trouble and conflict will always be with us. Our kids' surface reactions to trouble and conflict may be greater because they are hurting more intensely. Unless the loss of the absent parent is fully grieved, everyone is more on edge, more apt to lash out, hurting others in the unit, or internalize the pain, hurting the self.

Sometimes the unit cracks so often and so deeply that a crevasse develops and everyone is on the verge of falling through. At these times, the only thing to do is to step back and try to regain a perspective.

- "God was with Daniel in the lion's den, and He will be with us."
- "It's only for _____ years (I count backwards from each child's eighteenth birthday). We can make it for that long."
- "It could be worse. There could be twelve of us instead of six, one hundred thirty-two interpersonal

relationships instead of thirty." (I had to use a cal-
culator to figure that out.)

Or you can call the local monastery and ask for a reser-
vation for the weekend. This is often my last resort, but I
should probably consider it earlier, before the situation
becomes unbearable.

Keeping a perspective is crucial, especially for crevasse-
type cracks. But what about the daily kinds of cracks, the
"Mom, he looked at me funny" kind?

Any one of the following scenarios happens in our home
on a daily basis:

- "Mom, tell him to quit walking into my room anytime he feels like it!" in a shrill, shrieky voice demanding immediate attention.
- "How come you're *always* on her side?" in a
  sobbing, desperate voice demanding immediate
  attention.
- "Mom, I'm getting sick of her mimicking," in a too-
  controlled, on-the-edge voice demanding immediate attention.

You know what I mean. Or maybe your kids don't say
these things? Is there a family anywhere that doesn't deal
with these daily traumas?

When they happen, if you are energetic and excited
about "Train[ing] a child in the way he should go, [so]
when he is old he will not turn from it" (Proverbs
22:6)—if teaching your child to love is your highest pri-
ority at the moment—then the following suggestions
may prove helpful.

The surface reactions resulting from a particular conflict

should be considered just that—surface reactions. We should take them seriously because they are indications of a deeper issue, but the deeper issue is what we ultimately need to address, not the surface reaction.

In uncovering the deeper issue, it's important to stay cool and not react to the kids' reaction. Once we react in like manner, we've lost our credibility and right to give input. We've failed to "redeem the time" (*see* Ephesians 5:16 KJV).

If possible (and sometimes it's not), we should aim for resolution. Relationship resolution is often more difficult than individual resolution. If we can focus on helping each child resolve his or her personal issues, relationship resolution may automatically follow.

Let's look at these three tips more closely.

Surface Reactions

At a soccer game recently, Merilee's coach casually instructed her to take off her barrette. It was secured squarely on top of her head, where the ball sometimes bounces. He walked away, expecting her to obey his simple request. He had no idea he'd uncorked Mount St. Helens, and when it blew, I would be the one to be buried in the ashes.

Merilee's eyes immediately filled with tears as she turned to me in horror. "I'm not taking off my barrette!" she shrieked. "My hair. . . ."

I shrugged, well aware of the situation and wishing I were anywhere else but there. The hot lava was bubbling to the surface.

"Guess you can't play, then," I began.

She ripped the barrette out of her hair, then frantically smoothed, patted, and pulled at each strand in that spot. I reached out to try to fluff it up for her.

"Don't!" she screamed, jerking away from me. "You're making me look like a monster!"

Which I knew was exactly what she felt like. Still, I was hurt; I'd only wanted to help.

Travis and Amber stood watching this scenario. Bless their hearts. For once they didn't speak the words on the tips of their tongues: "A monster, that's it. I knew there was a word for what you look like." That definitely would have pushed her over the edge and out of control.

She spent the entire game playing with her hair. I spent the entire game forgiving her for her surface reaction.

Children are certainly not the only ones who express surface reactions. We all do it. The important thing is to become aware of it so that we use these reactions as an opportunity to deal with the deeper issues that trouble us.

If we only spin around on the surface of a conflict, never digging deep enough to unroot the real issue, we waste everyone's time. The problems reoccur and everyone repeats the same sins. No one learns anything.

Merilee's surface reaction was anger at me when I tried to help, because she couldn't direct her anger at her coach. Since fear is usually underneath anger, it didn't take me long to deduce what the deeper issue was here. Merilee was afraid of looking so horrible without her barrette that everyone on her soccer team would disown her—reject her. That's a serious issue.

Unfortunately, we didn't have time right then to get into the real issue. I just kind of assumed the coach might not want to hold up the game because of Merilee's barrette trauma. But it helped me understand where Merilee was hurting, so I could more easily forgive her.

As parents, we don't deal so well with our kids' surface reactions most of the time. We see them as something to be punished. When they emerge, we give our kids spankings, send them to their rooms until they can quit arguing, take away the phone, TV, or car until they can "be nice."

Surface reactions are our friends. They indicate where we are in our growth process. But we must let them accomplish their purpose. We must allow them to reveal the truth about a situation and then move beyond them to the real hurt needing God's touch.

How do we do that when all we can see is flailing arms, legs, and emotions?

The Deeper Issues

What exactly are our kids' deeper issues? I see the deeper issues separated into two basic compartments: fears and needs.

Fears	*Needs*
Abandonment	Love
Rejection	Acceptance
Violation	Safety
Betrayal	Security
Control	Justice
Loss	Discipline

This is not an exhaustive list, but it gives us a good idea of what's at the bottom of the family's reaction to surface disputes.

I arrived home from work recently to discover my children playing a game of risk that momentarily made me a wild woman, even though I could see that they were all in one piece. (That isn't always the case. We have experienced a number of broken bones in our years together.)

"Mom," Merilee gasped as she rushed into the room from the balcony. "Travis held me over the edge of the balcony and pretended to drop me! I was scared to death!"

My mouth dropped open; I could feel my blood begin to boil and my heart contract (anger at my son and fear for my daughter), but before I could emote, Amber followed her older sister into the house.

"I thought it was fun." Amber shrugged casually. "I knew Trav wouldn't drop me."

"It was not fun!" Merilee screamed, on the verge of hysteria.

Travis appeared then, grinning sheepishly when he saw the look of terror on my face. "What's wrong? You know I wouldn't drop them."

"That's hardly the point," I said, trying to calm down enough to talk to Travis about the deeper issue.

What was the deeper issue? Of course, Travis wouldn't drop them.

First of all, as I listened to Merilee's side of the story, I was led to believe that Travis swept his sister off her feet and dangled her over the edge before she could protest. She did not choose this, therefore he violated her. She felt terrified—insecure, unsafe, abandoned, and out of control. What's worse, her feelings weren't cared for. He only laughed when she screamed. Lest you get the wrong idea about Travis, he's not a monster, a tormentor of children. He's actually a sensitive young man. But he loves to tease and often goes too far. I discovered later that he thought Merilee was having fun since she was laughing, too (out of nervousness, I'm sure), during the first few moments of this crisis.

Amber, on the other hand, ran into his arms, begging him to do the same thing with her.

See, Amber trusts her brother. She *knew* he wouldn't drop her. But then Amber is the kind of kid who runs for the high diving board the minute she gets to the pool. Merilee would never attempt a high dive. Amber climbs onto every railing she sees; Merilee stays far from the edge. Amber charges after the ball in soccer; Merilee stays her distance, afraid of getting hit.

I need to help Travis see the deeper issue here, so he can accept each of his sisters where they are in their individual stages of growth. So he won't contribute to Merilee's fears but will be a part of helping her learn to trust.

And I need to help Merilee see that she absolutely must make herself vulnerable to Travis (trust him with her feelings, that is). If she's truly scared, she must say so, not laugh and pretend she's not. If she is ever able to trust him with her feelings, she will probably trust him to hold her over the edge of the balcony. I'd better make sure my kids know that this game, no matter what the deeper issues, is out!

Or maybe I need to work on my fear and let Travis dangle me over the edge.

Resolutions

Resolutions to family disputes are always desirable but not always possible. We must face that reality first thing, so we're not always devastated and overburdened with the fact that the sun has indeed gone down on your kids' wrath (*see* Ephesians 4:26 KJV) and it's somehow your fault.

Try as you may, you failed to get your kids to love one another by sundown. It just doesn't always happen.

Let Romans 12:18 give you the assurance you need: "If it is possible, as far as it depends on you, live at peace with everyone." Most often, when I hear this Scripture expounded upon, I hear the last part emphasized. Let's emphasize the first two parts for once. *If it is possible. As far as it depends on you.* God is always willing to dispense His grace when things are *not* possible, when we do our best and *can't* make it work.

Fortunately, every once in a while, God's love abounds and resolution *is* possible. The kids decide that yes, they'll go the love route just this once.

What are the verbal signs of unresolved conflict?

- "I hate him."
- "I'll never forgive her for that."
- "I'm moving to Dad's for sure. I'm not living with that dork."

The above clues tip you off to disputes that need resolving. Sometimes, as single parents, we think our kids are at a disadvantage for not having the benefit of a nuclear family. Don't kids need to watch their moms and dads fight, then resolve the fight, kiss and make up? How will they learn how to fight?

Let's consider two things here:

- We don't need to teach kids how to fight; they do that quite well. We must teach them how to love in the midst of a fight.
- Many adults know less than or at least as little as kids do about fighting. They can as easily provide an unhealthy example as they can a positive one.

We can't keep using the lack of a two-parent family as an excuse. Our kids are certainly at a disadvantage, but how many two-parent families are truly functional, as God intended?

What we should not do when mediating between our kids:

- Take sides. *Everyone* has a subjective viewpoint, and everyone is entitled to his or her feelings about the situation.
- Make the disputers say "I'm sorry" when they're not or hug their adversary when they'd really like to choke the other party.
- Order them to quit fighting without providing an outlet for their feelings.
- Threaten to send them to their dad's, to Mars, or to a foster home.

Although deep hostility or even the time factor can make resolution momentarily impossible, ideally we should resolve disputes as they occur.

"Mom, he looked at me funny" can quickly accelerate into "Mom, I hate him!" if the dispute is left to run its course without mature guidance and direction. Not that parents are always mature. We're talking the ideal here.

Daily "he looked at me funny" sibling disputes are resolved by using the following steps:

- Evaluate the surface reaction. Is it fear? Anger? A sense of violation? What's going on?
- Allow the child to express gut feelings.
- *Together*, negotiate a resolution. Does someone's behavior need adjusting? Who needs to repent? Who needs to forgive?

If we attempt to resolve a dispute without listening to everyone's feelings, we get nowhere. In the next chapter, we'll discover how to direct the unit's feelings without letting everyone's emotions cause the unit to fly out of control.

10
YEAH, THESE ARE TEARS

Sharing Honest Feelings

Feelings, those inner, often uncontrollable, stirring move-
ments deep inside that can one moment lift us to heights
of ecstasy and the next moment plunge us into the depths
of despair. If as adults we seldom understand them and
only occasionally handle them well, where does that leave
our kids?

Because I don't have a husband with whom to vent,
my kids are the ones who get to share in the best
and tolerate the worst of my emotional expressions. I
am definitely not an emotionally repressed person,
and I don't believe in repressing my kids. Now you
should have a clear picture of what you might find, were
you to walk into our home on any given day. We spend
a lot of time and energy learning to lovingly direct
the feelings that are always (and I do mean *always*)
flying free.

As a single parent, I receive no feedback in this area

and find myself constantly wondering how we're doing. Feedback from my kids, though infrequent, is especially meaningful. I remember when Merilee brought a little colored picture book home from school after Mother's Day one year. Each of her classmates had drawn a picture on a page and finished the phrase, "I love my mother because. . . ." Duplicates abounded. "I love my mother because she takes me to the mall" was way ahead of any of the others, with varied pictures of kids and their mothers hand in hand at the mall. "I love my mother because she buys me toys." "I love my mother because she drives me places." "I love my mother because she cooks good food."

But Merilee's page stood apart from the rest, at least to me. She had drawn the two of us sitting on her bed (my head couldn't really be that big). At the bottom she had written, "I love my mother because she listens to my feelings."

That was a statement about how my child views me, a statement about our relationship, a statement that validates me as a mother: "You're doing something right," it whispers.

Why, out of everything she could have chosen, did she choose that one? Because listening to her feelings means I *care*. The feelings themselves, urgent and intense, begin to subside as Merilee basks in the dynamics of the happening on her bed; someone cares.

When we give our kids permission to have their feelings, when we listen and validate those feelings and then encourage the expression of them, we say loud and clear: You are important. I care about what's happening inside of you.

Why Feelings

Feelings issue from somewhere around the heart. They can bond two people or drive them apart. They tell us the truth and lie to us at the same time. They bounce us off every wall or simmer in one spot. They demand expression but often require repression.

Confusing? You bet. And the list goes on indefinitely. Feelings are our best friends or our worst enemies. How do we explain that to our kids? How do we keep the family from being controlled by its collective feelings? How do we embrace our feelings and make them work for us?

In our family, we have four expressers and two repressers. The expressers are learning to repress at times, and the repressers are learning to express—for the sheer sake of survival.

Feelings are God's gift to us, not to be ignored, handled, stuffed, or destructively expressed to others. We tend to drop feelings into two categories: negative and positive. We think of jealousy, anger, sadness, loneliness, fear, and so on as negative, and love, happiness, joy, and so forth as positive. I once believed this and was frustrated because there seemed to be many more negative feelings than positive. It didn't seem fair.

But now I know that feelings are neither good nor bad, neither positive nor negative, neither right nor wrong. They fall under one feeling umbrella—love. When each member of our family learns how to take ownership of his or her feelings and express these feelings honestly, we come closer to what God intends for those of us in community—loving one another.

I remember a time when no one in our family understood feelings very well. The repressors just kind of mumbled around, quiet and sullen, and the expressers flailed loudly and vehemently. Then every so often we'd hear a distinct explosion; a repressor had blown a cork. It was called survival, and we were all barely making it.

We are no longer in that mode. The goal is no longer survival. We've proved that we can survive, much to our dismay on the really painful days. The goal now is love, genuine, honest, and real.

In the survival mode, before feelings were directed and love was the goal, a typical painful single-parent-unit scenario at the dinner table might go like this:

Someone spills a glass of milk, a fairly common mistake. We could take care of it in two minutes, but not when everyone is hurting.

"You dork! Watch what you're doing! My mashed potatoes are soaked!"

"Oh, like you never spill milk or something! Like you're all perfect!"

"That's right. At least I've got friends. I don't sit in my room alone all day playing Nintendo because I'm a dork and no one likes me!"

From the other side of the table: "Yeah, I never get to play Nintendo. He's always hogging it."

From somewhere over by the window: "Pass the butter, please."

"It's 'cuz he doesn't have any friends."

"I do so." This comes out as a sob.

"Oh, now the baby's going to cry—"

"No more!" I scream as my stomach contracts. One more hurting word and I will totally lose it.

"He is a baby. He always cries."

"I do not." Sobs.

"Pass the stupid butter!"

Knowing I can no longer stand to listen to my kids rip-ping one another apart and feeling powerless to do any-thing to make them stop, I push myself away from the table. My chair clatters to the floor and I retreat to my room, the only place I feel safe to release my frustration. A place where my kids can't hear my agony. These kinds of feelings I want to protect them from. These kinds of feel-ings, expressed, would only add to the damage done by the divorce.

In the kitchen, the voices grow louder and more angry. In my bedroom, the pain I bear for both myself and my kids drives me slowly crazy.

Now, a few pain-filled years later, the scenario starts out much the same but ends very differently. Someone spills a glass of milk.

"You dork! Watch what you're doing! My mashed po-tatoes are soaked!"

"Oh, like you never spill milk or something? Like you're all perfect!"

"Hold it," I order firmly. "Of course, no one's perfect. But there are no dorks in this family, either." I point to the spiller. "You clean up the milk." I point to the spillee. "You can clean your plate and get a new one."

If this doesn't settle it, we have to acknowledge the under-the-surface tension and deal with the real issue. The real issue may be unresolved feelings for the sparring partner, or it may be something a teacher did that day. It may even be something I did. I can't keep on top of ev-erything, that's for sure. Feelings have a way of staying pushed down inside us, and then, like a jack-in-the-box, popping up when we least expect it.

We're embarrassed by our feelings, for good reason.

Ever since we can remember, someone somewhere has been telling us:

- "Stuff it!"
- "Quit crying."
- "Be strong."
- "Don't be so sensitive."
- "What a baby."

Do you remember anyone in your childhood giving you permission to feel? To not be okay? To be weak? To cry for anything less than someone's death?

I don't.

Tears

"Dad gets upset 'cuz I always cry when I talk to you," my wonderfully still-tender son told me as we talked long distance on the phone one night.

"You can cry anytime you want to," I affirmed him. "The reason you cry is that you finally have someone you feel safe with."

It was true. But it would have been easy to assume that Grant wanted me to feel sorry for him, so he would fake tears every time we talked. It made sense; he never cried any other time.

But I knew better. I knew my kid. He wasn't about to risk letting just anyone see his feelings; he'd had his heart trampled on one too many times.

A sensitive boy, Grant had always cried easily. But since living with his father, he had learned to repress his feelings, hide his tears. It saddened me.

Tears: friend or foe? They don't seem like our friend when:

- We want to appear strong and tough in front of others, yet tears are streaming down our face, betraying us
- We want to give someone the message, "I don't care—no big deal," yet tears are streaming down our face, betraying us
- It's important that we repress our emotions so that another person can't hurt us, yet tears are streaming down our face, betraying us

. . . and giving another control over us. That's the real issue, isn't it? Once we let someone see our tears, we've lost our power. We could get hurt. We already are hurt.

Unless we know how to use our tears to manipulate, to gain control of others. As parents, it's important that we discern the ones in the family who know how to do this, including ourselves.

"Mom, I want to move to Dad's."

The first time I heard these words, I could honestly feel my heart shatter into a million pieces. I scrambled to gather them together so I wouldn't totally crumble in front of my oldest son, who had just spoken these words so casually, with no emotion, no feeling. Where was his heart? I don't know when I've heard more devastating words.

How did I react?

- "Oh, sure, honey. I'll help you pack."
- "It's about time. I have too many kids as it is."

- "Great. I can finally get rid of that lizard of yours."
- "What a relief. Right before the teen years hit."

No, not at all.

I cried—real tears, real pain—for the real loss of my firstborn. I cried right in front of him, while he sat cold and emotionless, staring at the television.

As time wound down and his departure drew near, my carnal self considered revenge: Hurt him as much as he'd hurt me. Show him I didn't care. No big deal. One less mouth to feed. One less person to cause conflict in the unit.

Or: Pour on the guilt. Let him see me cry—a lot. Use my tears to make him feel so guilty, he wouldn't leave.

No, I was already too committed to love, not survival. He wanted to go. At thirteen years old, he needed to go, to find the father he'd lost. I needed to let him.

So, because I wanted him to know how much I loved him, I sometimes let him see my tears. I refused to close my heart, even though I wanted to many times to stop the pain.

Other times I hid my tears of self-pity, anger, and pride, the grieving Gethsemane kind of tears that would only scare Travis, who was too young to understand them.

Travis left.

But there is an epilogue to this story. After four years of living with his father, Travis is back now, of his own accord. I'll see my firstborn graduate from high school this year.

And yes, this is a time when he will see my tears and share in them. They are now tears of gratitude, and no, he probably still won't understand them. Who can truly understand a mother's tears for her child?

Repression

When do we start repressing? When we're throwing a two-year-old tantrum and a "wise" adult tells us, "Stop that. You're acting like a two-year-old"? Is there something wrong with two-year-olds?

Or is it when we're twelve and we overhear a "wise" adult refer to us in a disgusted tone. "Puberty! She's going through puberty. I'm going to lock her up until she's twenty-one!" Is there something wrong with twelve-year-olds?

Or maybe it's when we're fifteen and we hear about the "terrible teens." Is it ever okay to be who we are?

How many of these damaging statements are we recycling to our kids? And we wonder why they don't talk to us.

We must all repress at times. When I can't handle one more "expression" in our home, I'm the first to scream, "Stuff it!" At least for now. And, of course, our kids can't go around school every day erupting in anger or crying about every little thing. It's not appropriate. Yet, as we've pretty much established, kids aren't all that concerned about what's appropriate. Besides, who sets the guidelines for what's appropriate? How come adults always get to decide what's best for kids? As adults, can't we ever just offer guidance, then step back and let our kids make decisions for themselves? Is it up to us to always decide when kids can and can't express their emotions?

These are important questions.

I happen to believe that it is my responsibility as my kids' parent to discourage repression of emotions and encourage honesty in acknowledging *gut* (we use the word *gut* for emotion and feeling) feelings and love for others in the expression of those feelings.

Expression of emotion is not the goal—love is. That's how we discern when to express and when to repress. Sometimes it's loving to express, sometimes it's loving to repress—or maybe the right word here is *suppress*.

"What's wrong, honey?" I ask Merilee, who is lying facedown on her bed, her body rigid as a lamppost. She is clutching a pillow, definitely in a repressive posture.

"Noflin'," her muffled voice answers.

This is a wonderful relief: She doesn't want to talk. Merilee always talks. Merilee always expresses emotion. Merilee bounces off every wall, colliding with the rest of the family at regular intervals. If she wants to repress today, I think I'll let her.

Dwight, at the other extreme, rarely expresses his emotions. When he does, he doesn't do it kindly or quietly, but I let him, because I'm so glad to finally know what he's thinking and feeling. After the explosion, we talk about what it means to speak the truth in love (Ephesians 4:15).

If you have a repressor in your unit, the following may help you.

Take the Repressor Out Alone

In our family, we have something called "Night Out." Once a week I take one of my kids on his or her night out. A repressor will often emotionally open up when no one else is around.

Assure the Repressor That Feelings Are Valid

The sensitive child may have gotten hurt in the emotional realm at some point. Make sure your child knows feelings are acceptable.

Ask the Repressor Feeling-Oriented Questions

The repressor may be emotionally out of touch and need help in feeling his or her feelings.

Assure the Repressor of Your Love

A child may repress because he or she feels unsafe. Discover the cause of the fear and begin to build a loving foundation underneath the individual as well as the relationship.

Affirm the Repressor When Honest Feelings Are Expressed

When the repressor does take the risk, be sure to encourage any attempts, successful or not. Each step is an important one.

A repressor can become an expresser. Oh, dear. What would I do with five expressers? I'm glad God supplies grace in abundance.

Appropriate Expression

Appropriate is such a boring, stuffy word. To use it when discussing what's best for kids amuses me for some reason. I can just hear Travis mimicking the word in his stuffiest English-teacher voice: "Appropriate."

I remember a time at work when some creative employees and myself made a list of the worst words we could think of and spent the afternoon shouting them back and forth to one another. Words like *discipline, submission,* and *responsibility* headed the list, followed by *obedience, diet,* and *moderation.* I know *appropriate* was on the list somewhere.

So, for lack of a better word, I use the word *appropriate* in teaching our kids when and when not to express their emotions. But I use it loosely. In this context it simply means there are good times and not-so-good times for us to express ourselves.

It is not appropriate for Merilee to climb (literally) all over Amber in anger because Amber took one of her sister's tapes without asking. Nor is it appropriate for Grant to sulk in his room for hours because Dwight got a new jacket.

So what is appropriate? Or maybe we should ask, what is loving?

It is both loving and appropriate for any child at any time at any place to cry out with emotion.

- "I'm mad!"
- "I'm jealous!"
- "I'm sad!"
- "I'm lonely!"
- "I need—"

We want our kids to get in touch with their feelings and needs. What often ends up being inappropriate and unloving is the aftermath of getting in touch. Maybe you've noticed this in your family. Kids don't simply express the feeling or need—they take action. How do we teach them to clothe themselves "with compassion, kindness, humility, gentleness, and patience" (Colossians 3:12)? They laugh at me when I use words like these, so I pray them more than speak them.

There are no right and wrong ways to express our feelings; there are only loving and unloving ways. But who cares about being loving to someone you're so mad at that you're spitting nails? That's the tricky part.

When Travis moved back into our home after being gone to his dad's for four years, Merilee did not handle it well. She'd held the position of oldest for a while and was used to getting much of my attention. Overnight she became cranky, self-centered, and supersensitive to just about everything everybody said to her.

Travis, not fully understanding the dynamics, played right into the situation, generally doing all he could to keep Merilee irritated and upset. Nine-year-old Amber, confused by her sister's behavior, leaned toward Travis's side, which only aggravated the situation and made Merilee more angry.

After a few weeks of this, I was exhausted, so one night I took Merilee to Dairy Queen, plunked her down in front of a hot fudge sundae, and laid it out.

"I am done," I announced. "It looks like I'm the only one in this family who's even trying to love, and I can't do it by myself. Either you get on board or it's every man [*and woman and girl*, I added to myself. I hate sexist language] for himself."

"You mean—love Travis?" she asked, as if I'd just suggested she hug a rattlesnake.

"That's right. No matter what. No matter how he acts or treats you."

"Oh, wow." She was obviously in excruciating pain just thinking about it.

"Remember: If you decide not to, you're on your own."

Lest you think I was being horribly harsh, I'd already talked to Travis. He was with the program; I knew she wouldn't get slaughtered.

"Love him no matter what?" she repeated. "Even when he makes fun of Danny [her rock star hero]? Even when he threatens to drop Teddy [her hamster] off the deck?"

I nodded and waited. Time marched on. The hot fudge sundae melted. It grew dark outside.

Merilee sighed. "Okay, I'll try." She spoke these words as if she were sealing her fate forever, about to be burned at the stake, risking her very life. Someday I would enroll her in an acting class.

Vulnerability in Relationship

I had asked Merilee to make herself vulnerable to a brother whom she had no reason to trust at the moment. That was asking a lot.

Do we have the right to require vulnerability from our kids in their relationships with one another? When they don't feel safe? I once heard a well-known writer and speaker say on public television that vulnerability is the greatest risk we take in life.

That's so true, because we have no guarantee that another will respect and/or treasure our feelings. We risk every time we open our hearts and show our feelings.

I have reached a place of authenticity in my life where I can no longer hide my true self, whether I'm with my kids or anyone else, and I desire this same kind of authenticity for my kids. The key word is *desire*, not require. I can want this for them—I can't demand it.

Vulnerability in relationship must be earned. I'm human. If my kids choose not to cherish my feelings, I pull in. And they do the same with me. Yet at other times I must sacrifice my personal emotional safety to teach and train them about authenticity, integrity, and being real, whether or not anyone in their world values these traits.

God's ideal, I'm sure, is to provide the family structure as a place of safety for children. Two parents should create a nest of security out of which their children will eventually fly to create nests of security for their own young. But seldom does the ideal work out the way it's supposed to. Nothing can create more insecurity for a child than the abandonment (deliberate or not) of a parent. Can a child ever really let down with the remaining parent when the very real fear of abandonment is always prevalent?

Three weeks after Travis moved back in, Merilee confessed: "I feel alone. You're always talking to *him*. I don't see you anymore. We don't talk like we used to. I'm so jealous."

Did I take on guilt, defend myself, and get mad at her? Did I feel overly responsible for her feelings? Did I treat them lightly, telling her to lighten up? No, because it was one of those times when Merilee's openness was a blessing; I didn't have to guess what was bothering her.

"You know, there's a story in the Bible called the Prodigal Son," I began. "Now Travis isn't exactly a prodigal, but. . . ."

She listened closely, her wheels and heart turning.

". . . he did leave to seek his inheritance, in a way. When the prodigal returned some time later, he was broken, beat down, sad."

Merilee nodded.

"His father, standing at the door, saw him coming from a long way off and ran to meet him. They hugged. The father was so happy, he threw him a big party." (I wonder if the prodigal son's father was a single parent. The parable doesn't mention his mother.)

Merilee smiled.

"But the elder brother was jealous. He'd stayed home with the father the whole time and never been given a party. But the father said, 'Let's celebrate. Your brother was lost and now is found.' "

Silence.

"You've always been here. You know I love you. Now Travis is home. Can we celebrate? Have a party? Just for a few days?"

Merilee understood. She had chosen the vulnerable path, and all was well—at least for the moment.

11
I DON'T CARE WHAT OTHERS DO (OR HAVE)

Winning the Comparison Game

"Mom, are we poor?"

"It's all relative," I answer, hoping that will satisfy this child but knowing it won't.

"Oh, so it's their fault?"

"Whose?"

"Our relatives."

"No. Actually, well, it's like this. . . ." But how do I explain it?

"I know. It's 'cuz we don't have a dad." Arms across chest, frown in place, body rigid. "If we had a dad, we'd have money and stuff."

The truth is we have more money and nicer possessions now than when we were married. But the kids were little then and didn't care as much. Now, as some of them have entered their teens, what we own matters a great deal and makes a statement about who we are.

It's not just money and possessions, of course. We're also inferior and "weird" because we don't:

- Have a dad
- Take vacations to Hawaii, Europe, or the Caribbean
- Eat dinner at six o'clock like normal people (we eat when I feel like cooking)
- Have a dog
- Live in a house (we live in an apartment at the moment)
- Have an extended family: grandparents, uncles, aunts, and cousins

Why do I emerge out of every one of these conversations feeling as though everything we don't have or do is all my fault?

And what about what we do have?

- Caring friends with whom we share holidays and celebrate birthdays
- Three hamsters
- A microwave and a new van
- A swimming pool, tanning salon, and hot tub in our apartment house
- Healthy bodies (we're hardly ever sick)

How easy it is to take what we do have for granted and miserably focus on what we don't have.

The Comparison

My kids, presently nine, eleven, thirteen, fifteen, and seventeen, are still under the delusion that life is fair. I'm not sure when they started believing that myth or why. I know I've never taught them that.

God never said it, either. Paul tells us in 2 Corinthians 10:12: ". . . when they measure themselves by themselves and compare themselves with themselves, they are not wise."

However, as with being appropriate, since when do kids care about growing in wisdom?

Why are kids so anxious to compare our family with another, and why do we never measure up? I see a number of reasons for this tendency:

- Someone is unhappy because someone doesn't have something or can't do something.
- Someone wants to blame someone else because someone can't have or can't do something.
- Someone is greedy, always wanting to do or have more.
- Someone is insecure and too conscious of the areas in which the family is "weak" (*weak* is used subjectively here).

I hate to admit this, but one reason kids fall into the comparison trap is that we adults program them to. I've often wondered how it is that I ended up divorced with five kids when so many of my friends get to stay married (some of them even happily so). My mother died recently. So how come so many of my friends get to keep their parents? How come every ounce of food I eat turns into a pound of fat, when many of my friends seem to be able to eat whatever they want? How come?

Comparing ourselves with others is a normal response to pain or insecurity. We want to make sense out of life's injustices. If we can make ourselves come out ahead or superior to others, we can boost our sagging egos. But it doesn't often work out that we come out ahead. The point here is that we can't expect our kids to grow in an area unless we can at least model for them.

Comparing ourselves with others may be normal, but it's not productive. We usually come out the loser and feel all the worse for it.

I was raised by a single parent. My mother remained single after my father died when I was five. I don't know if the following is in any way connected to the above information, but it does stick out in my mind. I remember:

- Having to wear a swimming suit two summers in a row. I was mortified. *Everyone* got a new swimming suit each summer.
- Being deprived of snow cones. My mother thought they were too messy. But didn't *every* other American child eat snow cones to his or her heart's content?
- Living in an apartment, not a house. *None* of my friends lived in apartments.
- My childhood without a dad—sad. Didn't every kid. . . .

Not really. Some kids are deprived of both parents, raised in foster homes, orphanages, or adopted. Some kids have abusive, alcoholic, or mentally ill parents.

Every once in a while—not often, but every once in a while—one of my kids says, "Oh, I'm so glad you're my mom. Jeremy's mom weighs five hundred pounds, I swear. That would be so embarrassing."

Or, "I would hate it if I had Gary's dad. Everyone has to be quiet all day 'cuz he works nights and sleeps days. He's a bear if he gets woke up." Then I get a grateful smile and a hug. I take a photo of my child's face so I can remember this rare moment of actual gratitude.

As I mentioned, I do believe the tendency to compare is normal. If our kids would just say, "Isn't it interesting that *all* my friends' mothers let them stay up past nine o'clock on school nights?" then "Isn't it interesting that one in a million make their kids go to bed at nine? Isn't that interesting?" I would agree, "Fascinating," and that would be that.

No, it's not the comparing itself that makes me crazy sometimes. It's the attitude or reaction that accompanies the comparison.

The Reaction

Whenever our kids compare themselves to others (or compare you to another parent) and come out wanting, it makes them very unhappy, to make a gross understatement. The common reaction is one of anger, jealousy, or self-pity. And I usually take the brunt of it, because I couldn't or wouldn't—even if I could—make myself any different just to make my child happy.

"Tiffany takes ballet lessons," Merilee told me one day.

"That's nice."

"She also takes piano lessons, and her mom's enrolling her in acting school this summer."

"Bully for Tiffany." I was starting to get the drift.

"She wore this new dress to school the other day. She told me her mother paid eighty dollars for it."

"Wow. Hope she didn't spill anything on it at lunch. Probably needs dry cleaning." I was trying to keep the conversation lighthearted.

"Tiffany gets whatever she wants. All she has to do is ask."

"Tiffany has *two* parents who work," I said through gritted teeth.

"Right. If we had two parents, a dad. . . ." She stopped at the fierce look on my face. "Or maybe you could get another job" was her helpful suggestion.

"I already have three." My fierce look had turned to one of exhaustion.

"I just wish we had more money . . . or something," she whined.

Why was money so important? We did have lots of somethings.

I wanted to provide everything my daughter wanted and needed. I couldn't do it; it was impossible. I was only one person doing the best I could. I sighed. "I'm sorry we don't have more. It must be frustrating for you to have so little when you want so much."

"It's the most horrible thing about my life," she quickly agreed. Eleven-year-olds often exaggerate their pain. But one's pain, just like one's financial position, is relative.

I remember one day a few years ago when my kids and I shared the same experience but our reactions were diametrically opposed.

We had moved to Seattle the day before and were going grocery shopping for the first time in our new neighborhood. As we pulled into the store's parking lot, I happened to glance across the street and immediately cried out in pure delight.

"You guys—look! Value Village!"

Value Village, a thrift-store chain, was a familiar and welcome sight. I'd shopped there regularly back home for my kids' clothes and other household necessities. The sight of this old friend reassured me that I could still bargain hunt for my kids' clothes. It also began to make Seattle feel like home.

I hardly had a moment to relish these thoughts, though, so deafening were the groans from the back of the station wagon.

"Not Value Village!"

"Oh, no."

"How embarrassing."

"Let's get outa' here."

"What's wrong with Value Village?" Three-year-old Amber couldn't figure out what all the commotion was about. It was nice to still have at least one member of the family who wasn't worldly-wise. I could still give all the burnt cookies to Amber when everyone else turned up their noses. She didn't know any better.

I had recently begun to notice my kids' protests and resistance to shopping at Value Village, but I think I chose to stay in denial, knowing I couldn't afford new clothes as my marriage was breaking up. We were fortunate to have food enough for one day. More often than not, we didn't.

"You guys don't like Value Village?" I asked weakly.

Guffaws, loud laughter, near hysteria.

"Mom, really. . . ."

"Are you kidding? Everyone's leftovers?"

"Yeah. I remember that time Jason [Travis's friend] got rid of a pair of junky plaid pants and Mom brought them home from Value Village for me."

More loud laughter.

Where had I been? How had I missed this turning of the tide? No matter. With or without my knowledge, it had turned, and I would somehow have to deal with the debris on the shore.

"From now on, I'm not shopping anywhere but Nord-strom," Travis announced.

Now it was my turn to groan.

We didn't buy many clothes that first year in Seattle; then Travis moved to his father's. Surprisingly, his father bought him what he wanted—at Nordstrom.

Unfortunately, Travis started a trend that has endured to this day, five years later. Nordstrom or nothing. Even Amber has caught on. She has to wear what's "in style."

Many single parents—or any parents, for that matter—might say, "That's ridiculous. Those kids need to be taught the value of a dollar and that they can't have everything they want."

So true. My kids are in want most of the time, for since they insist on shopping at Nordstrom, they get only a few select pieces compared with the volumes we used to get at Value Village. It's their choice; to each his own. And they're learning the value of a dollar. At seventeen now, and back with me, Travis earns his own money and buys all of his own clothes—at Nordstrom.

Why Nordstrom? Because Nordstrom has the "popular styles." Since I remember the trauma of having to wear the same swimsuit two summers in a row or the ridicule of the kids who wore Wrangler jeans instead of Levis, I know the issue of clothes is no small deal.

Without a dad, my kids already have too many strikes against them. I'll allow them the clothes.

The point is, reaction always follows comparison. Whether it's anger, envy, self-pity, or something else, the reaction must be confronted and the truth put into perspective.

The Truth

What is the truth in all this? I don't know if there is one truth in the area of comparison. I think we can deduce several:

- God loves all His kids the same.
- Our unit is unique and has unique needs.
- Because the real motive behind our comparisons is often to point out to God, or anyone who will listen, how unfair everything is, we can count on feeling worse after the comparison.
- Comparing usually won't change a situation.
- God is more concerned about how we respond to the injustices and inequities of life than He is about whether or not we all get a fair shake.
- God's love for us is not determined by what we have in life, whether it's a dad or a Nintendo game.

We can rely on the above truths, but does knowing these things make any difference when we're tempted to compare?

Let's take these truths one at a time and look at them more closely, starting with a probing question for each.

If God loves all His kids the same, why are some so rich, some so poor, some so beautiful, some so ugly, some so smart, some so dumb, and so forth? Try to explain this one to your kids. It makes no sense.

Some people are rich because they've worked hard and earned it; others because they were born into a wealthy family. Some people are beautiful because they wear lots of makeup and have face-lifts and hair implants; others were born good-looking. Some people are smart because they've worked hard in school; others are born with lots of brainpower.

Remember the story in Luke 19:11–27? To me, this story illustrates my point. It's not what God gives us that's important; it's what we *do* with what He gives us.

In my five kids I have a potential professional athlete, a dancer/singer, a mechanic/carpenter, an artist/engineer, and a psychologist. The gifts are evident. The only aspirations I have for my kids is that they grow in love and use their God-given gifts to love their world. This would please God, would please me, and ultimately would bring great contentment and satisfaction to my kids, for I believe we're the most fulfilled when we're doing what we were created to do.

We do great damage to our kids when we try to live out our shattered dreams through their lives. Our life is ours—separate from theirs.

Dwight, my potential artist/engineer, has been interested only in skateboarding for the last three years. Recently, I was pleasantly surprised to discover that, all on his own, he's been buying different kinds of pens and markers and privately drawing in his room. At fifteen, he may have finally realized there's not a lot of money in skateboarding, but I'd like to think God is talking to him.

What makes our family unique? What makes us any different from the millions of other households around the world? Just as we know that no two snowflakes or grains of sand are alike, so we know that God created no two people or combinations of people alike.

I do know this truth. That's why when my kids begin to compare their sad state of affairs to a classmate's (or classmate's parent's) "perfection" in the same area, I see it for what it is: a detour. It has nothing to do with our situation.

The fact that Mr. and Mrs. Wonderful let little Susie Wonderful stay up until ten o'clock on school nights has absolutely nothing to do with us. Or because Mr. and Mrs. Moneybags bought Johnnie Moneybags a three-hundred-dollar mountain bike doesn't mean Mrs. Chisholm must run out and do likewise.

The above two items of interest simply mean that one, some, or all of my five kids want(s) to stay up later and/or get a new bike. That's the issue. That's what we'll discuss, pros and cons, regardless of what the Wonderfuls and Moneybags did yesterday or will do tomorrow.

What does motivate comparison? Pain. Greed. Discontent. Ingratitude. Demandingness. Insecurity.

It's a waste of time to address and haggle over the comparison itself. What we need to confront is the underlying need motivating the comparisons.

When Merilee begs me to let her stay up until ten o'clock on weeknights and uses as ammunition the fact that Susie's parents let her, what is she really saying? She wants me to take note of the fact that she's eleven now, almost twelve, and deserves more respect and some special privileges.

I keep telling her that maturity and responsibility go along with special privileges. I'll think about letting her stay up later when she stops pushing the nine o'clock bedtime every night.

"But that's not fair," is Merilee's plaintive cry.

Maybe not, maybe so. Put in perspective, it's neither fair nor unfair; it just is.

If comparing makes us feel worse and doesn't often change a situation, then why do we continue to do it? It helps to understand that comparing is simply an expression of pain or frustration, a cry for attention or justice.

Merilee might as well cry, "Ouch! Ouch!" as "Susie gets to stay up until ten o'clock." The same thing would be accomplished, although the latter does have some blame mixed with it and might make her feel a little better if she could hold me responsible for her pain.

What Merilee doesn't understand is that the new knowledge of Susie's privilege doesn't make me immediately say, "Oh, well, that changes everything. If Susie gets to stay up, of course you must, too."

If anything, it has the opposite effect. I don't like to be manipulated.

Why is our response to life so important to God? Because it reveals who we are at the moment and who we are becoming.

I would guess our response to life and its challenges falls into three main categories:

- A passive stance, where we stand in one spot screaming "Aaaaargh!" and let life's waves crash over us, wreaking havoc
- An aggressive charge forward, where, flailing and kicking, we drown in three feet of water
- A confident position of waiting and being before doing, as together with God we navigate life's challenging waters

As God leads us, we must lead our kids in response number three.

When we moved a few months ago, we had to sell much of our furniture and belongings to pay the bills. My girls ended up without a bed, since we had to return their bunk beds to their original owner. This was a serious state of affairs, and the comparisons began.

"Lisa has a canopy bed and a matching dresser."

"Everyone has a bed. I'm so embarrassed."

I had to agree with her. In America, everyone had beds, except perhaps the homeless. What to do? Sit around and feel sorry for ourselves? What would be our response to this dilemma?

As I searched the want ads in hopes of finding temporary employment to get us over the hump, my eyes fell on an ad for phone book deliveries. Not a very prestigious job.

But then I decided it was about time my girls realized that nice things do cost some bucks. And in order to buy nice things, one must exert oneself—in short, *work* for these bucks.

I swallowed my pride, and the following week found the three of us traipsing from door to door, phone books slung over our shoulders. In a few days we earned the down payment for the beautiful, cozy, brass daybed that my girls are enjoying today.

We earned the money together, and I think God just might have been proud of us.

If God's love is not determined by what we do or don't have, what does determine it?

I remember another move some years back. I received a card from a friend after we'd moved into our new beautiful split-level home.

"God must love you a lot," it read. "Look at all He's done, all He's given to you."

I remember clearly my reaction to those words written by my well-wishing friend. *No!* I cried out inside. *This house is not a sign of God's love. It's a wooden structure, that's all. If this is God's love, my heart is overflowing with too many tough questions.*

What about my single-parent friend who lives in a little

shanty on the edge of town? Does God love her less because she lives in a shanty?

What about right after my divorce when we had to go on public assistance for a while in order to survive? It was four years before I could talk about this without great shame. Did God love me less then than He does now?

No, we can't itemize our material goods or evaluate our financial status and thereby measure God's love in cups or liters.

God's love is unconditional, consistent, always and forever, whether we live in a mansion or a shanty. It was determined once and for all in one magnanimous historical event. "This is how God showed his love among us: He sent his one and only Son into the world . . ." (1 John 4:9).

Into the *world*. God poured all of Himself into all of the world when He hung Himself on a cross in the form of man. It makes our puny comparisons look petty.

Still, there are those times when even Jesus' death on the cross seems to lose its daily relevance when it comes to surviving the ongoing crises of the single parent. How do we deal with those high-stress times of wanting to cash it all in and walk off the set?

12
I QUIT

When Going On Means Giving Up

One thing we might as well realize about being a parent: It goes on and on and on. . . .

That's not necessarily true about being a single parent, for every once in a while, some poor unsuspecting soul happens along, falls madly in love in spite of the munchkins, and marries one of us. Then we desert the ranks and enter the category of *un*single parenting, which goes on and on and on. . . .

But since no poor unsuspecting soul waits in the wings to slip a ring on my finger, and since I'm not looking, I guess I'll resign myself to the role of single mother for the next few years.

Actually, the other day I quit. It was one of those days. You know the kind. Chubs, the hamster, disappeared, the VCR stopped working in the middle of *Batman*, and our only bottle of syrup had ants floating in it.

Anyway, when the kids broke the laundry-room door, I quit. I stopped picking up after them, refused to cook dinner, left the house, and didn't come home for two hours.

When I finally did return home, I dramatically slammed the door for effect and called out, "Well, I decided to come home after all."

"Shhh," Grant mumbled as he frantically pressed the buttons of his hand-held video game. "I'm almost on the third level."

They hadn't even realized I was gone. The piles on the floor had grown by at least two feet each, the smell of burned noodles hung in the air (who said they needed *me* to cook dinner?), and the broken laundry-room door had fallen into the bathroom mirror. Batman was poised in the air on the TV screen in the same position as when I'd left, and I heard rustling noises in the kitchen—a sure sign that Chubs was somewhere nearby. The dramatic statement of my quitting had gone completely unnoticed.

Sometimes I quit for five minutes, sometimes for an hour or longer. Once I quit for a whole day, but I took my kids with me; I just wasn't their mother for that day.

Remember that book with the wonderful title that came out a few years ago: *Where Does a Mother Go to Resign?* I never have read the book, but I haven't forgotten the title. The reason I didn't read the book was that I knew it probably wouldn't apply to me, since I'm not just a mother. I'm a *single* mother.

Maybe a place does exist where a mother can go to resign, but a single mother doesn't have that option. A single mother can't resign; there's no one around to take over while she's gone.

Oh, every once in a while I indulge in a particular dialogue with myself: "Well, I've been at this mothering thing now for seventeen-plus years, alone for seven, and I've come to the conclusion that it's just not for me. I guess it's not my calling, after all. It's time for a career change."

Or, "I deserve a break. Mothering is stressful, after all. I think I'll take a two-year sabbatical in Europe. If the job's still open when I get back, maybe we can work out some terms."

Or, "I didn't realize those sweet little babies would one day become kids and teenagers. This isn't fair; no one read me the fine print. I wonder if I can return them to the hospital and make some kind of a trade? Maybe the hospital has a recycling program."

By the way, if my kids ever read this book, they'll know I'm just letting off steam. I wouldn't trade any one of them for the cutest, sweetest baby in the world, the same way they wouldn't trade me for June Cleaver. At least, I don't think they would.

I never tell my kids I'm quitting, of course. They would feel rejected and unwanted. I love my kids—I want my kids—just not every single moment.

So when I quit physically and leave the house, they assume I'm off to the store or on a drive. If a glassy look comes into my eyes, meaning I have emotionally and mentally checked out, they simply assume I'm into a new book or thinking adult thoughts that they wouldn't be interested in anyway.

In all seriousness, one of the most, if not the most, difficult things about single parenting is its dailiness. The pressures and responsibilities are heavy on us when we fall into bed each night, and they're still there when we wake up in the morning. Personally, I believe they're on us while we sleep, too. I dreamed recently that bunches of earwigs were attacking me. After I relayed the dream to a friend, he asked me if I was feeling "bugged" by lots of little things. (I don't think he meant my kids.)

Definitely. Not to mention lots of big things.

My kids are always showing up in my dreams, too. I remember one where I was about to climb into my car to go somewhere and all five of them climbed into the front seat with me! Do I need to interpret that dream?

Yes, as single parents, we can definitely feel crowded, unable to breathe, trapped.

Trapped

The trapped feeling descends when we feel we have no choices, no options. We're stuck, with no escape or exit in sight. Have you ever felt trapped on a carnival ride, and no matter how loud you screamed, you knew it wasn't going to stop (as a matter of fact, your screaming prolonged the ride, because they have sadists running those things)? Yes, it does stop, but only after you're totally hysterical.

If you're not totally hysterical at the moment, it's good to remember that living with kids means hysteria is never that far off. Or it could mean you've gone slowly and quietly over the edge. Keep in mind that 1 Corinthians 10:12 tells us if we think we're standing firm, we must be careful we don't fall. And then that wonderfully comforting verse that follows: ". . . God is faithful; he will not let you be tempted beyond what you can bear. But when you are tempted, he will also provide a way out so you can stand up under it" (1 Corinthians 10:13).

Warning: In the paragraph preceding the above, we see that the way out is not sexual immorality (23,000 Israelites who tried that died in one day!), testing the Lord (the

Israelites who tried that were killed by snakes), or grumbling (the complainers were killed by a destroying angel) (*see* 1 Corinthians 10:8–10).

I really wonder how the single parents in ancient Israel made it without grumbling! If we still lived under the law, the destroying angel would have finished me off the first time I griped about the ring around the tub.

Now that we know what the way out isn't (and I'm sure the above is not an exhaustive list), what is it?

The way out of that intense trapped feeling comes to us in different forms:

- Your ex goes temporarily insane and invites all the kids over at the same time.
- You win a one-way trip for *one* to a remote island somewhere.
- You suddenly get a perspective and start laughing. Careful here. Remember how close you are to hysteria.
- Your kids miraculously fall asleep before midnight.

If God says He'll provide a way out, He will—momentarily. Kids have a way of hanging around until they're eighteen or thrown out at twenty-five.

Though you may often think otherwise, all we really need is a temporary way of escape, time to catch our breath.

No getting around it: Kids are an endurance test. We all know the Scriptures about enduring to the end and all that. I would put any single parent up against Rocky; he'd have himself quite a match.

The trapped feeling is normal. It comes and goes. Too long without relief, though, and it leads to the "I quit" syndrome, another normal reaction to life with kids. Is it really ever okay to quit?

Legitimate Quitting

Earlier in this chapter I mentioned that I quit once for an entire day. Life had become a bit much to handle, both at work and home. I walked into work one day, began crying even before I got to my desk, turned around, and walked back out. I cried all the way home.

Why was I going home, anyway? It was summer, and my kids were all home and bored. Fights broke out constantly. The pressure would only be worse at home.

"God, I quit," I sobbed. "I can't do this, even one more day. I need a vacation—even if it's just for a day."

God, in all of His wisdom, seemed to say, "Take it."

So I did. The kids met me at the door, bored, fighting, and tattling, as I knew they would. But it didn't bother me, because I was gone on vacation. I laid the rules for the day down immediately.

"We are going on a mini-vacation," I announced to my brood.

They looked at me as if to say, "Another of Mom's crazy schemes," but, intrigued, they waited to hear the rest.

"Just for today I'm not anyone's mother. Did you hear me? That means you can't tell me your problems, no tattling—nothing. I'm not your mother today. Got that?"

Amber, five at that time, looked a little confused, but everyone else seemed to understand.

We all piled into the van. The first stop was to get us all a balloon. Balloons set an atmosphere. We walked around Green Lake; Grant hunted frogs while the rest of us fed the ducks. We drove into downtown Seattle, where we walked up and down the pier, eating ice-cream cones. We went to the aquarium. We ate dinner at an all-you-can-eat Chinese restaurant. Just for the day, I paid no attention at all to what anything cost. Neither did the kids, I might add.

We laughed and played together for one whole day. The trapped feeling lifted, as did the pressure and stress.

When I get to the point of wanting to quit, it's not my relationship with my kids I can no longer handle, it's the responsibility I feel to deal with all their problems, as well as my own. With the responsibility lifted for that one day, even if it was only in my mind, I was free to enjoy my relationship with my kids.

I believe single parents, in order to save their sanity, must allow themselves occasional times of quitting.

Here are a few legitimate quitting ideas:

Trade children one day a week with another parent as interested in quitting as you are. I did this for many years before my children were all in school. I took a friend's kids for one day, and she took mine for another. I guarded my one day a week with my life. It saved my sanity more times than I can count.

Take separate vacations. Couples who take separate vacations are the brunt of many jokes, but I would no more consider going on vacation with all my kids than I would consider going *anywhere* with all my kids. Unless your kids absolutely adore one another (and that would make me suspicious) and adore you, as well, it's emotional suicide to take everyone on vacation. Anytime we all climb into the van and go across town, we emerge rather traumatized on the other side. I'd hate to think what would happen after a week or so.

I take at least two vacations every year: one by myself or

with a friend and another with one or, at the most, two of my kids (the ones who are farthest apart in years or the ones who like each other the most).

Find a nanny. For room and board, some nannies will work cheap. It may be a high school or college girl who needs a place to stay or an older woman who needs to be needed and would love your kids to pieces. Then when you quit, someone will be there.

Plan regular times of roller skating, swimming, or movies, and drop the kids off. Don't feel guilty every time you don't go *with* your child to a lesson, session, practice, or movie. Try to schedule your quitting around these outings so you have time for yourself and can relax, knowing the natives are occupied.

Remove yourself when the cork is about to blow. This works out best when you can see the steam rising before the cork blows, but sometimes you just don't know you're as stressed out as you are. You may not be able to wait for God to provide the way of escape or believe that He will. It's healthier for you and your kids if you leave the scene rather than stay to say and do damage that you'll regret later.

Quitting is sometimes necessary. Don't feel guilty about it. Find a legitimate way to quit. In the meantime, inside of us are untapped resources that, if we can learn to plug into them, will decrease the stress. The urge to quit will come less often.

Resources

All the vehicles that drive us into single parenting—a spouse's death, divorce, rape, or the simple knowledge that we won't be marrying our baby's father—are guaranteed to push us into overload. Most single parents are already stretched out to the max at the beginning because of the traumatic circumstances surrounding their new role. My kids lost their father at the time of my divorce, but they didn't have much of a mother, either. I spent most of my days for the first few years crying or artificially anesthetizing the pain. My resources were depleted at the start.

I had no inner resources because my relationship with God lacked a foundation. I had to accept His unconditional love and believe that He had good gifts for me: grace, mercy, comfort, peace, joy, and faith. These were all just lifeless words in the Bible until I realized that the Holy Spirit desired to breathe life into each gift and use them to strengthen and empower this broken, wounded child of God.

If applied, the following steps may help you tap into your inner resources:

- Acknowledge the emotions (anger, grief, fear, blame) connected to the initial event that thrust you into single parenting. It most likely was not your choice.
- Allow yourself to express these emotions either to God or a trusted friend or both.
- Forgive the ones you see as responsible for your situation—probably God and the man you no longer have or want.
- Begin to live one day at a time, receiving God's gift to you for that day alone, trusting you will have what you need for tomorrow when tomorrow comes.

As we receive God's strength, we can teach our kids to tap into their own inner resources so they are not always using up ours but are relying on their own gifts from God.

Recently, Merilee went through a difficult period where she couldn't sleep alone at night. Whenever she closed her eyes, she saw a particular monster from a television program she'd watched some months ago. She had to sleep with the lights on and she became hysterical every time her younger sister, with whom she shared a room, spent the night at a friend's.

"What does he look like?" I asked her once.

She described him and I thought, *Yipes! I'm sleeping with the lights on, too!* Fortunately, I got a grip before she saw my reaction.

I tried sleeping with her, praying with her, soothing her before bedtime. I finally got frustrated because no matter what, she always ended up blaming Amber or me (instead of the monster) for her night misery. We could never make it better, so it must be our fault.

One night after we'd had a lengthy discussion and gotten nowhere, I was exhausted. Even though she was still crying and miserable, I said, "I'm going to bed. I can't help you. You won't believe anything I'm telling you."

I had told her that:

- The monster was only in her mind, therefore couldn't attack or hurt her physically
- God was in the room and in her heart, and He was stronger than the monster
- She had power and control over the worst that could happen to her—her own fear

. . . and many more truths, none of which she let penetrate.

I threw up my hands. "It's up to you now. I give up." I went to bed. I couldn't *make* her believe the truth; she would have to exercise her own faith.

I found out the next morning that I'd done the loving thing by going to bed. As long as I was there believing for her, she didn't have to believe for herself. As soon as I left the scene, she had no option but to use her faith and take charge of the monster. She did, and he's never returned since.

Monsters are basically all the same, whether they come in the form of the responsibilities of single parenting or as an imaginary green blob of pulsating flesh like the one in Merilee's mind. Their function is to torment us and distract us from God's real purposes for our lives. But as we learn to appropriate God's inner resources, we can reduce our monsters to their proper size.

Darkest Before Dawn

You know the old saying, "It's darkest before dawn." Well-meaning people say this to encourage us. So we hopefully wait for the dawn, because we know it can't get any darker.

And it gets darker.

"I can't do this anymore!" you scream.

But your friends have their own problems, and your kids just look at you blankly. "Did you say something, Mom?"

The world continues to revolve, your kids' needs continue to grow greater, the pressure continues to mount.

I know one single parent who discovered she had life-threatening asthma (one attack almost killed her), her ex-husband cut off her child support, and she had to move from her home—all in one week. Unfortunately, many people get asthma. Ex-husbands (and wives) are always getting behind on their child-support payments. And everyone moves now and then. But you put all that on a single parent whose responsibilities are already overwhelming, and you have one huge basket case whose basket is unraveling rather quickly.

Where is the dawn? Dawn is not the day your youngest child leaves home. Nor is it the possible someday in the future when you stand at the altar and pledge your love forever to someone who will help carry your load. And dawn is definitely not the day you land the dream job that pays you so much money you can hire a private nanny, tutor, chauffeur, gardener, and housekeeper.

No, dawn is the day you finally realize you can't do this, after all. It's too much. You quit. To quit in this sense is not what we've been talking about—it's not to give up in despair. This kind of quitting is to surrender, to quit trying so hard to be more than the human you are. It has to get really dark for some of us single parents before we reach this place. We're a proud lot.

But only when we reach this place of surrender can God renew our vision.

Renewed Vision

It's easy to lose vision when all we seem to be doing every day is dragging ourselves and the kids out of bed in the morning, dragging ourselves to work, dragging ourselves home after work, dragging ourselves into the kitchen to cook dinner, dragging ourselves around the kitchen and the rest of the house for the remainder of the evening, and dragging ourselves and the kids to bed at night.

Will the pep ever return to our step? Will life ever be more than dragging ourselves around?

It's entirely up to you and me. In other words, it's our choice. That fact alone should offer us some comfort.

I "quit in despair" for the first four years I was a single parent. I ran from the responsibilities and from my precious little ones, who needed me.

In the game of hide-and-seek, there are those who hide and one who seeks. During my four years of running, there was only one who hid and five who sought. This version wasn't fun, though, because the seekers never found the one who hid. I wouldn't let myself be found, no matter how many little voices cried, "Mommy, where are you?" I numbed myself to their cries and wallowed in my own pain.

It was a day to celebrate when I finally "quit in surrender" and let myself be found by both God and my kids. The family had suffered while I was gone, and God and I had a lot of work to do to make it functional again.

To God, my surrender meant:

- The prodigal daughter had come home.
- The walls had crumbled, leaving me open to receive all the gifts He'd longed to pour into me for so long.
- The beginning of the family's healing.

To me, my surrender meant:

- No more running. I could finally relax and enjoy both God and my kids.
- No more struggling just to survive. The family would soon throb with life.
- A reuniting with my kids. I didn't realize until I was back how very much I'd missed them.

To my kids, my surrender meant:

- Undivided attention. I could now give them my all without feeling sucked up by their needs.
- Heartfelt hugs. I could now hug them without feeling swallowed up and desperately clung to.
- More time. I could now give them hours at a time, knowing I would always have time left over for myself because I deserved it and would make sure I got it.

If you're at the point of quitting, go for it. It may be the most loving thing you'll ever do for your kids.

Is it possible? Can we actually survive the single-parenting ride without casualties? And not just survive but grow healthier as individuals and more loving in relating to one another?

Read on.

13
LOOK! WE'RE DOING IT!

Life Goes On

As I write this final chapter, it's New Year's Eve, and I'm sitting in a Japanese teahouse in the university district of Seattle with no date. New Year's Eve and no one to kiss. I'll be forty this year. Where is my life really going? What have I accomplished? I'd love to be in love, but no, I haven't started looking, and I think my kids have given up hope that I ever will.

I'm always thrust into my annual panic attack as New Year's Eve nears and I have no plans. Every year on New Year's day I announce to whoever will listen, "This will never happen to me again. Next year I will have something to do—something exciting, exotic, adventurous."

And every year it happens to me again. I have nothing to do. My kids always have plans. They have plans tonight. Dwight and Grant are with their father; Merilee is at a church service with her best friend; Amber is swapping and dealing Nintendo games (yes, I finally bought a Nintendo for my kids for Christmas) with her best friend;

Travis has rented two movies and is watching them on our VCR (the other large package under the tree) with his best friend (himself). Okay, they're not really exciting plans, but they're happy.

The panic peaked tonight at about seven o'clock, when I realized how alone on the planet I really am. I mean, if you don't have a date on New Year's Eve, you have to be the most rejected person on the planet. It's tragic.

"I can't believe this has happened to me again," I wailed as I grabbed some bread out of the refrigerator and slammed the door so hard the magnets all fell off.

"What?" Merilee asked timidly. "What's wrong?"

"What do you mean, what?" I yelled. "What do you think? It's New Year's Eve, and I don't have a date." I paused. "I want to kiss someone," I explained further.

"But you have no one to kiss," she reminded me.

"That, thank you, is exactly my point," I said as I shook my finger in her face. I did not want to talk to Merilee about this.

She felt bad, I could tell. "You could have kept that nerdy guy—"

I knew she was only trying to help. "He had buck teeth." I slapped a couple of slices of avocado and some turkey on a piece of sourdough bread.

"Yuk!" She turned up her nose. I didn't know if it was because of the buck teeth or the avocado and turkey sandwich. I was beyond caring. "I mean, here I am, almost forty years old, living with my kids—"

"Thanks a lot," Merilee interrupted.

"—in an apartment in Lynnwood. Not even Seattle, mind you, but Lynnwood, with no one to kiss."

Travis appeared in the kitchen, a big grin on his face. He never took me seriously. No one ever took me seriously.

"All that was okay yesterday," he said.

"Well, it's not okay today," I fumed. "I hate my life."

"Let's rent *Dead Poets Society* tonight," Travis optimistically suggested.

Of course. For Travis and me, this movie was the cure for all of life's ills. But I knew that tonight not even *Dead Poets Society* could help. The theme "Seize the Day" would only remind me of how unseized this particular day was—of how unseized my life was.

God, what now? I prayed silently as I drove Merilee to her friend's house. *I know we've been here before, but just remind me. What makes life worth living if you're not loved on New Year's Eve?* Tears burned in my eyes.

I said the cordial "Hello. Thank you for taking Merilee tonight. Call me tomorrow when you want to get rid of her" to Merilee's friend's mom. And then a strange thing happened.

"I love you, Mom," Merilee whispered as she got out of the van. Merilee seldom says that, and I don't know if she ever says it first.

Stunned, I said, "Yeah, I love you, too." But she was already running into the house.

I *was* loved on New Year's Eve. Maybe not by who and in the way I thought I needed, but I *was* loved.

No, I may not receive many kisses. I may not always be understood or paid attention to. I may not even always be liked. But I *am* loved. What else really matters on New Year's Eve or any other day?

Just as many things are essential for a plant to grow or a flower to bloom—sunlight, water, nutrients—so are many things essential for love to bloom and grow. Ingredients such as kindness, gentleness, a sense of humor, and vulnerability are some of those things. In our family,

I've found that a VCR and Nintendo are essential, or my love for the other members becomes suspect.

But I see four major ingredients to ensure our ongoing love for one another. We've referred to them off and on throughout this book. Those four things are acceptance, forgiveness, encouragement, and a spiritual commitment. Without any one of them in operation at any time, the unit begins to disintegrate.

Acceptance

A typical conversation at the dinner table or in the car may include the following:

"You're going out of the house with that huge zit on your nose?" (Implying unacceptable ugliness.)

"Mom, I want you to drop me off a block away. I don't want anyone to see me in our orange Pinto." (Implying unacceptable poverty.)

"You don't even know what we're talking about, so just keep out of it." (Implying unacceptable stupidity.)

As we've established many times in this book, a kid's measure of someone's worth is usually based on looks, financial status, and/or intelligence. Everyone, of course, has their own variations of these three categories. Where do they get their belief systems, anyway? Have I unconsciously taught them the above? Yes, I do admit, I like to be thought of as attractive, financially well-off, and intelligent. But have I elevated these attributes to a place in my kids' thinking where they don't belong? Or can I blame the media or my kids' peers? It's probably a combination. No matter.

The important thing is that I have to somehow resist that line of thinking and promote acceptance of one another regardless of looks, financial status, or brainpower. Who or what am I resisting? The media. The school system. My kids' peers. Society. Myself.

Myself. I hate to admit how locked into that mentality I am myself. I am too often turned off or on by the way people look or how well read they are. I hate that tendency in me, especially when it conflicts with the way I believe about loving others unconditionally.

So I work on it and help my kids to work on it, even when they don't see the necessity. The only way I know how to help my kids work on anything is through example. When I blow it in front of my kids and find myself judging instead of accepting, I admit it.

A few unspoken guidelines keep us on track. In our unit we get to:

- Be who we are
- Feel what we feel
- Choose what we want

. . . as long as we are committed to loving God and others as we love ourselves (Matthew 22:37, 39). Since I don't lay down rigid rules about what unconditional love and acceptance look like, I must stay alert and evaluate each situation for itself.

When Travis can't accept Merilee because her hair "sticks up funny" or when Grant thinks Amber's friend Tonya is a "dork," that truly is Travis's or Grant's problem, not Merilee's or Amber's. Why should Travis care what Merilee's hair does or Grant care if Amber hangs out with "dorks," "geeks," or "nerds"? What difference does it make?

Unless I want to go into the complicated and often confusing principles of co-dependency with my kids, I'm left

with the simple truth of God's Word: "Accept one another, then, just as Christ accepted you, in order to bring
praise to God" (Romans 15:7). That's pure and simple and
uncomplicated. But is it easy? No, it's impossible.

Can we really do this, after all?

Forgiveness

Forgiveness, the second ingredient necessary to ensure
that we make it together in some kind of an ongoing way,
is one I know my kids wish I'd never heard of. Their
philosophy: "It all blows over eventually, so why try to
jump start the relational process with forgiveness?" (I'm
paraphrasing here.) I used to think that kids were much
better at this forgiving business than we "mature" adults.
They don't tend to harbor and nurse the hurts the way we
do. After a short period of time, the victim seems to be
able to relate well to the one who inflicted the pain. But I
am re-evaluating my original idea on that. Now I wonder
if kids are just much better at repressing their hurt; they
still have plenty of room on their pile of wounds, unlike
we who have been stacking for decades.

One reason I am re-evaluating is that I'm listening more
closely to my kids' feelings when they're hurt. Forgiveness is making a choice to let go of pain caused by others;
it is a process that culminates in loving others in a deeper
way. I don't particularly see my kids moving through this
process unless it's initiated by me. What I do hear and see
when a wound is inflicted:

- "He *always* does that. He's *never* nice to me."
- "There's no point in talking to her. I've tried. She
  never listens."
- "It happens *every single time*. I don't care anymore."

Hyperboles and judgments abound, a sure sign that someone is piling up accusations and blame. Forgiveness has not yet been activated. Well, I have to admit, forgiveness is not often the first thing I'm eager to offer when I'm hurt. "Oh, boy, so-and-so just hurt me. Now I get to forgive." Not at all. So I'm not faulting my kids. The only difference between my kids and me is that I've lived long enough with myself and others to have experienced firsthand more times than I can count the results of nonforgiveness and the benefits of forgiveness. God really did know what He was doing when He gave us the guidelines for relating to one another. "Be kind and compassionate to one another, forgiving each other, just as in Christ God forgave you" (Ephesians 4:32). If we truly think about it, receiving God's forgiveness for our sins is a wonderful privilege. How can we dare withhold it from one another?

But how to explain this wonderful privilege to my kids remains the great challenge. Especially when they come back with (and this is a regular occurrence): "Mom, I'm not like you—into forgiving everyone all the time. You're the only one I know who's always going around forgiving everyone." And the look that follows says, "C'mon, get with it. It's the twentieth century, a dog-eat-dog world. You won't survive unless you learn to bark and bite like the rest of us."

Or: "So where has kindness, love, and forgiveness ever gotten anyone? You're going to get walked on—mangled." This comment was made by one of my kids after a lengthy discussion that I initiated on God's purpose for putting us here on earth together: to love one another. Yet, just a few days later, I watched this same child, who had argued until the bitter end of the discussion, correct a friend who was acting in an unloving and unforgiving way toward others: "If you really want to get into this God thing, you're going to have to learn how to love people." They may not admit it to me, but I believe God's truths are lodging somewhere in their hearts.

Just the other day Amber told me that she and Merilee actually hugged each other after a fight—all on their own! This little bit of news nearly sent me into cardiac arrest. Amber said, "Mom, it felt major good to hug Merilee!"

Encouragement

To encourage is to hearten or to give courage to—one more thing our kids aren't all that interested in. But I believe it's crucial. Without it, you have one discouraged unit.

Why is it that kids rush in from school and the first thing they do is spout off all the negative and depressing things that happened that day?

- "David threw up."
- "Kelly got sent to the principal's office."
- "Rachel called me a ————."

"Anything good happen today?" I might ask.

"Can't think of anything." Pause. "Oh, yeah, I stood up to that bully, Sam, like you told me to. Smacked him a good one. Here's a note from the teacher about it."

Could our kids possibly be programmed? If so, couldn't they be reprogrammed? I've often wished that when we make the decision to love God and others, that's exactly what would happen. Like turning on a light—zap—we would be loving, caring, encouraging people. It just doesn't work that way.

Besides, there's a lot to be discouraged about:

- Wars and rumors of wars
- Worn-out tennis shoes
- Higher gas prices
- A shortage of men
- Late child-support checks

It's not much better from a child's point of view:

- Divorced parents
- Worn-out tennis shoes
- Poverty (no hot tub or big-screen TV)
- Custodial parent's lack of time, attention, and energy
- Disagreeable and impossible siblings

Personally, I have to *decide* to look beyond all of that every single day and find something encouraging. "But encourage one another daily, as long as it is called Today, so that none of you may be hardened by sin's deceitfulness" (Hebrews 3:13).

As a single parent in God's world, I must *choose* to transcend discouragement whenever I can. I must choose to appreciate:

- My child's smile
- Paid bills, sometimes even on time
- A date—any date
- My child's hug
- Five minutes to myself

The challenge? To teach our kids how to encourage others, including their parents, by grabbing God's perspective, even if it's only for a moment. Let's teach our kids to:

- Look for the sunbeam between the clouds
- Hear the music in the discord
- Wonder and question in a world that has all the answers
- Look for the stream in the desert
- Listen for God's voice in the midst of chaos

And with these gifts, may they encourage their world. May we encourage one another.

Spiritual Commitment

I do believe that the only way a single-parent family can survive and thrive is for each member to make an individual decision to love God and live for Him as He illuminates the path. And He will.

Spiritual commitment is much more than reading a Bible story together every night and saying a "Lay me down to sleep" prayer. It also means:

- Leaving the last piece of pie for someone else
- Sacrificing one's favorite sitcom to attend a boring school program
- Remembering to ask permission before wearing someone else's blouse or shirt
- Getting off the phone when someone needs to make a call

. . . and more.

Does this make sense? What do the above have to do with God? Plenty. ". . . whatever you did for one of the least of these brothers of mine, you did for me" (Matthew 25:40). When we love God, we love His kids, and vice versa. Loving God's kids is to love God.

For me, making a spiritual commitment means to:

- Love God and people, i.e., my kids
- Act like it occasionally

It means to check in with God regularly, especially in those areas where I really have my own ideas as to what's best for the family.

For how long? For forever. We will always be a family, no matter how old anyone gets or how far away anyone moves, because spiritual commitments to spiritual relationships are eternal, the only thing we take to heaven with us.

I wonder how we can help our kids to see the importance of all this stuff. Travis got his first car last week, a fairly new shiny black Volkswagen GTI. One week and two tickets later, it's a *wrecked* shiny black Volkswagen GTI. That's what he's concerned about. Dwight is concerned about perfecting his new skateboard trick. Grant's concern? His new bunnies. Merilee's latest concern is where to hang her newest rock star poster. And Amber is concerned about how to get the prize out of the cereal box.

That's today. Tomorrow will bring new concerns for all of us. It's how we live.

But in between all of these concerns we talk about God and His enduring love for us. We remember that the Son of God was a little kid once, sometimes lonely and sad— human, like us. We know that He wants to share our lonely, sad, and happy times, that He's committed to us as we are to Him and to each other.

We Can Do It

"What are you doing?" I cry as I stare at the yellowish orange glob of cheese dripping down over the sides of the bread and spreading out onto the griddle.

"Making a grilled cheese sandwich," Merilee answers indignantly.

"But I was just going to make dinner."

Slam! I watch Travis stride through the apartment, kicking off shoes and dropping hat and duffel bag as he goes.

"Where were you? You could have at least left a note," I remark.

"Oh, didn't I leave a note?" He scratches his head.

"Where's Amber?" I ask.

"She was here a minute ago." Splat! Merilee turns her cheese sandwich. "Maybe she went to Dana's."

"She knows she's supposed to tell me where—"

The phone rings. "Hi, Mom, it's Grant. Hey, I got a girlfriend. Can I tell you about her? And then Dwight wants to talk. I think he needs some money for shoes."

But these two don't even live with me at the moment. No matter. They're part of the unit, and I care tremendously about them. And the beat goes on—with all of us. It's called life. It takes a lot of courage to live nowadays. Can we do it?

I think maybe we can. I think maybe we are. We don't do it very well at times, but we do rise to the occasion, because we're a family.

Travis summed it up well the other day. When I asked him why he didn't treat us in the unit at least as well as he treated his friends, he answered, "If I'm mean to my friends, they'll take off. But I know that when I wake up every morning, you guys will still be there. You're always there." He looked sheepish. "I'm sorry."

He's right. We'll always be there. Because deep down we love one another. Do we take one another for granted? Maybe. I suppose we could work on that a bit. I could include a chapter on that in this book, but I smell a grilled cheese sandwich burning.

Life really does move on.

"Huddle up, you guys. We're all we have."

"But I'm cramped."

"I'm hot."

"I'm bored."

"Can I go to the bathroom?"

"Later. Right now, let's hold one another."

Who needs a date on New Year's Eve? Who needs money in the bank? Who needs an exotic summer vacation? I've got all I need right here: God and my kids.

"Hey, Mom?"

"What?"

"I love you."

A taste of heaven.